San Francisco
CURIOSITIES

Help Us Keep This Guide Up to Date

Every effort has been made by the author and editors to make this guide as accurate and useful as possible. However, many things can change after a guide is published— establishments close, phone numbers change, hiking trails are rerouted, facilities come under new management, etc.

We would love to hear from you concerning your experiences with this guide and how you feel it could be made better and be kept up to date. While we may not be able to respond to all comments and suggestions, we'll take them to heart and we'll also make certain to share them with the author. Please send your comments and suggestions to the following address:

Globe Pequot Press
Reader Response/Editorial Department
P.O. Box 480
Guilford, CT 06437

Or you may e-mail us at:
editorial@GlobePequot.com

Thanks for your input, and happy travels!

Curiosities Series

San Francisco
CURIOSITIES

Quirky characters,
roadside oddities &
other offbeat stuff

Saul Rubin

Guilford, Connecticut

The prices, rates, and hours listed in this guidebook were confirmed at press time. We recommend, however, that you call establishments to obtain current information before traveling.

To buy books in quantity for corporate use
or incentives, call **(800) 962–0973**
or e-mail **premiums@GlobePequot.com**.

Copyright © 2010 by Morris Book Publishing, LLC

Photos by Saul Rubin unless otherwise noted.
Maps by Sue Murray copyright © Morris Book Publishing, LLC
Text design: Bret Kerr
Layout artist: Casey Shain
Project editor: John Burbidge

Library of Congress Cataloging-in-Publication data is available on file.

ISBN 978-0-7627-5867-8
ISSN 2154-2872

Printed in the United States of America

10 9 8 7 6 5 4 3 2 1

To my intrepid travelers and loves of my life,
Bethany and Naomi, and our many trips
to San Francisco, a favorite destination

San Francisco Overview

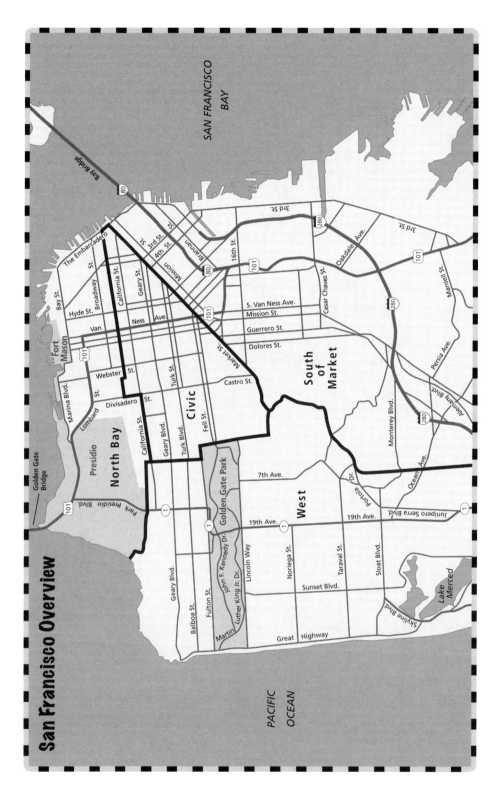

contents

★ ★

introduction

★ ★

A massive earthquake and devastating fire like the one that struck San Francisco in 1906 would have been a deathblow to most cities. But not San Francisco, where residents exude high-energy and exuberant spirit. Chalk it up to the bracing climate and hilly terrain, which demand a hardy populace. Or maybe it's just great coffee.

Less than a decade after the earthquake, the city mounted an impressive world's fair, the Pan Pacific International Exposition, to proclaim its recovery. San Franciscans have never looked back.

San Francisco has always gone beyond what other cities would do. The city uses outdated modes of transportation such as cable cars and nineteenth-century trams that other cities long ago discarded.

San Franciscans are creative. Television was invented here (bet you didn't know that) as well as the mai tai and fortune cookie.

This is a city that loves its wild animals, which love the city back. San Franciscans embraced a swooping bird in the Financial District that dive-bombed and pecked at the heads of passersby to protect her fledglings' nest in the summer of 2009. She was affectionately named Swoops, and her antics became a popular attraction. The famed wild parrots of Telegraph Hill endeared themselves to locals. They don't really hang around Telegraph Hill much anymore—now they're enjoying all parts of the city. The barking, foul-smelling sea lions that took over several docks at a San Francisco wharf might have been shooed away by the citizens of more narrow-minded cities, but they have been embraced by San Francisco at Pier 39.

All of these stories are recounted here, and so many more.

Just a note about how the book is organized before you jump in. San Francisco is a city of many neighborhoods, but this book divides San Francisco into four sections: Civic, North Bay, South of Market, and West. The Civic chapter includes the Civic Center, Nob Hill, the Financial District, Union Square, and Chinatown. The North Bay includes North Beach, Fisherman's Wharf, Russian Hill, the Marina, Telegraph Hill, and the Presidio. South of Market includes the Mission District, Mission Bay, SoMa, Potrero Hill, the Castro, Noe Valley, and China Basin. And West includes Golden Gate Park, Lincoln Park, Haight-Ashbury, and the Sunset and Richmond neighborhoods.

1

Civic

San Francisco's cable cars are quaint, romantic, and a great tourist attraction. But let's face it, they're also slow-moving road hogs that creak and groan as they lumber around town.

San Francisco's stubborn insistence on nineteenth-century technology in a twenty-first-century world reveals a city marching to a different drummer, or a whole other type of music. The slow joyride on a cable car sends a message that it's not about rushing from one place to another but about savoring each stop along the way.

That's good advice for this densely packed section of the city, which offers so much eye candy and offbeat spots for adventure. There's a national forest in an alley of a downtrodden neighborhood (just use your imagination), a tiki bar where it rains inside, and a darkened theater of sound. There are nineteenth-century Italian trams to board, and throwback trolleys to ride that other cities long ago discarded. You can hop on a cable car, or head over to the Cable Car Museum where all the secrets behind the city's trademark form of public transit are revealed. The museum is also a working powerhouse where you can see the actual cables hard at work.

The Wells Fargo Museum features several of the company's coveted "treasure boxes" that tantalized a whole generation of highway robbers. The museum also offers a shocking exhibit for San Francisco—a stagecoach that dates to 1852. Huh? An outdated form of transportation on display in a museum and not shuttling people around the city? It's, well, so unlike San Francisco.

★ ★

The Stuff Publicity Is Made Of

Upstairs at John's Grill, one of San Francisco's oldest restaurants, a bird with a menacing glare gazes out from behind a closely watched glass display case. Actually it's a statue, and it's not just any bird. It's the Maltese Falcon.

No, it's not *that* Maltese Falcon. You know, the one from the noir film based on the classic Dashiell Hammett detective novel of the same name. The movie ends with Humphrey Bogart waxing poetic as he refers to the mysterious bird as "the stuff dreams are made of." And it's not even a replica of the movie prop bird. The restaurant had

Sure, it looks like the real Maltese Falcon, but don't believe it.

✦ ✦

one of those, but it was stolen in 2007 in a still-unsolved caper worthy of any Hammett work.

No, this bird is actually a replica of a replica of a replica—a plot with enough twists to satisfy any crime story buff. Considering that the original Maltese Falcon of Hammett's creation, a bird statue encrusted with jewels, turned out to be a leaden fake, this falcon may really be the stuff that nightmares are made of.

All deception aside, John's Grill offers an honest tribute to the famed book, film, and the book's creator. Hammett dined here in the 1920s while working as a detective before starting his literary career. He worked John's Grill into his fiction, writing one sequence in *The Maltese Falcon* where his detective hero, Sam Spade, walks into the restaurant and orders up some chops, a baked potato, and sliced tomatoes.

The venerable restaurant has played up its Falcon connection with menu items related to the work, including the Sam Spade Lamb Chops and the specialty house drink, the "Bloody Brigid," named for the femme fatale who did in Spade's partner.

An upstairs Maltese Falcon shrine includes a dining room with walls adorned with framed movie stills and dialogue from the film. Outside the upstairs room you'll find the display case with the falcon statue, as well as books related to Hammett, including an original copy of *The Maltese Falcon*.

The current statue was completed by students and teachers at the San Francisco Academy of Art University at the request of restaurant owner John Konstin. It's bronze with an intimidating look, just daring any would-be thief. Go ahead and stare back at 63 Ellis Street. For more information call (415) 986-3274 or visit www.johnsgrill.com.

A Race That's Way Off Course

Thousands of people spend hours getting in the right condition to run in the annual Bay to Breakers race. To some that means drinking plenty of beer, or perhaps something Polynesian with rum. To others it's designing an improbable costume more appropriate for Mardi

Gras than a footrace. It doesn't matter, because most entrants aren't trying to win. Their primary goal is to look fabulous as they cross the starting line. There's not a care about how they'll fare at the finish, or whether they'll even get there.

The Bay to Breakers is a moving carnival in sneakers. It's also the world's biggest road race, setting a record with 102,500 runners in 1986.

Some people who enter actually care about winning the race. These racers prepare by practicing their running—training that would never occur to the majority of the field. This elite crowd speeds along the course, which starts downtown and ends at the ocean along the Great Highway, finishing in about thirty-five minutes. Meanwhile, many runners are still at the start, bunched up with thousands of others. In some years it takes up to ninety minutes for everyone just to cross the starting line.

And what a sight it is: thousands of people outfitted in outlandish costumes. There are people dressed as everything from vegetables to San Francisco landmarks. There's a team of spawning salmon who run backwards while wearing fish outfits. One year a man came dressed in drag while carting two small Victorian houses behind him. Lots of people wear bathrobes to this morning competition. Some women jog along in full wedding regalia. To others, clothing is optional. A growing number of people opt to run naked, a tradition known as the Bare to Breakers.

Victory for most folks is not how fast they get to the finish but how many times along the way they're asked to stop and pose for pictures.

The race, held each May, began in 1912 as part of efforts to boost community spirit after the 1906 earthquake. It was run as a conventional race for decades until costumed runners began lacing up to join in the 1970s. Things have pretty much gotten out of hand ever since.

Smooth Operators

An unheralded feat of memory was exhibited in the early 1900s inside a stylish pagoda structure in Chinatown. This building, at 743 Washington Street, once housed the operators of the Chinese Telephone Exchange.

The operators had to memorize the names and numbers, and even the addresses and occupations, of up to 5,000 Chinatown residents who were part of the exchange. On top of that, they had to be fluent in English and up to five Chinese dialects.

The exchange was heavily used by Chinatown residents to connect with one another before dial phones came into vogue in the 1940s.

A Whole Lotta Shakin' Going On

One day in 2008, friends Kevin Whittaker and Cory Jens greeted each other in San Francisco the way most people do: with a handshake. Fair enough.

But then the pair got a little carried away and kept on shaking hands—for the next nine and a half hours. When they finally let go, they had set a new world record for hand shaking.

While some might consider the achievement dubious, Whittaker was obviously proud, telling the *San Francisco Chronicle:* "It's epic because it's the first time this has been done in human history."

The pair persevered through challenges such as how to avoid overly sweaty hands and using the bathroom and imbibing refreshments at a bar while still engaged in shaking hands.

★ ★

Planting Seeds in a Seedy Neighborhood

Darryl Smith remembers driving around the Tenderloin District in San Francisco as a kid with his dad, a policeman, who told him, "You don't ever want to find yourself here."

That was probably sage advice, considering that the Tenderloin is a densely populated neighborhood with more than its share of the homeless, wandering drug addicts, and overall urban blight.

Of course, make something taboo for a kid and that's the first thing he'll want to do. So as an adult, Smith, an artist, found himself occupying a Tenderloin work space overlooking a typical alleyway

Darryl Smith tends to the Tenderloin National Forest.

for this neighborhood—a stark place of strewn garbage and bare concrete.

Smith dreamed of better things, which is a credit to his artistic imagination. And then he made it happen.

It started with the planting of one redwood tree. And now the alley has been transformed into an ecological and artistic oasis optimistically called the Tenderloin National Forest, located in Cohen Alley off Ellis Street.

The alley is now filled with a variety of plants and trees, providing a stunning green space to counter the bleak urban landscape just outside. Artists have adorned the surrounding walls with colorfully majestic murals, and there is a central hearth where people can gather for events. Even the ground has been turned into an art project, decorated with stone mosaics meant to mimic basket designs of the Ohlone Indians from the San Francisco Bay area.

"We saw an opportunity to integrate art and ecology," is how Smith explains the transformation of the alley.

The alley includes a small hut made of mud and straw surrounded by drought-tolerant plants. There's a wooden rowboat whimsically perched atop a pile of red bricks against a wall painted with a vibrant portrait of a family.

Visitors are welcome here Wednesday through Saturday from 11:00 a.m. to 3:00 p.m. The forest is maintained by the Luggage Store, the art gallery Smith founded and today directs with Laurie Lazer. You can check out the gallery's Web site (www.luggagestore gallery.org) for information on cultural programs scheduled at the forest or call them at (415) 255-9571.

They Keep Going and Going

Most public transportation officials look ahead to new, sleeker ways to move people around. But not in San Francisco. The city famed for its cable cars prefers old, clunkier forms of public transit.

That's the only way to explain the city's major investment in its

Old railcars aren't allowed to retire in San Francisco.

F-Market & Wharves line, which features vintage streetcars, some
dating to the late nineteenth century.

Operated by the San Francisco Municipal Railway, the line opened
in 1995 with service between Castro and Market Streets. It was
extended five years later to run all the way to Fisherman's Wharf.

Pay a regular MUNI fare, and step into vintage streetcars that
other cities might employ as exhibits in a transportation museum.

Many of the cars are known as PCC streetcars, built in the 1930s
and introduced in many American cities by transit officials as a way
to compete with cars and buses. San Francisco spent more than half
a million dollars to restore each car. Then it decorated them with
designs used when they were first in service in cities like Brooklyn,
Philadelphia, Baltimore, and Boston.

The line also includes vintage Italian trams and streetcars from Russia, England, Portugal, and other far-away places, giving these antiques new life in twenty-first-century San Francisco.

The line is the world's longest running vintage streetcar line in daily service. Cars operate daily every ten minutes or so from 6:00 a.m. to midnight.

The city even employs a streetcar named *Desire,* acquired in a trade with New Orleans, which received a vintage California Street cable car. Of course what this vintage 1923 car may desire at this point is retirement, but that's not allowed in a city where old work-horses are expected to keep chugging along.

No Feeding of Feathered Movie Stars

If you feed a wild parrot in San Francisco, you're subject to a fine. In 2007 the city passed an ordinance making it illegal to "feed or offer food to any red-masked parakeet" in a city park.

The law underscores the city's strong feelings for its flock of wild parrots, celebrated in a 2003 documentary, *The Wild Parrots of Telegraph Hill.* Bird lovers believed the law necessary to protect the birds and make them find food themselves.

The cute South American birds with the phosphorescent green bodies and scarlet heads are spotted all over the city, no longer just in Telegraph Hill. So look, take pictures, but don't offer any nosh.

★ ★

Ring Leaders Set the Tone for This Contest

San Francisco may be the only city instantly recognized by a noise—in this case, the familiar clanging of its fabled cable cars. Knowing how to properly sound the bell is as important to cable car operators as knowing how to make the cars stop and go—probably more so in this tourist town where the people who drive cable cars are just as much performers as transportation workers.

The bells are there for a purpose and not merely for the entertainment value of providing a jaunty soundtrack for a tourist visit. They are primarily used to communicate signals between the car's gripman and conductor. One bell toll from the conductor tells the gripman to stop the car. They're also sounded as warnings to pedestrians to get the heck out of the way because a cable car is coming.

But enough of that. What matters most to professional cable car bell ringers are style points. That's why each year they square off in a fiercely contested battle to determine the city's best cable car bell ringer. Contestants get a minute to sway judges with their originality, style, and overall technique. These unique concerts sound a bit like pieces of silverware rhythmically dropping to the floor.

The contest dates back to 1949 when the city held a competition to select three gripmen to operate a cable car at a Chicago railroad fair. Annual contests were started in 1955, discontinued during the 1960s and early 1970s, and started up again in 1977. They're held each July in Union Square.

All That Jazz about Religion

When Bishop Franzo King saw the great saxophonist John Coltrane perform in San Francisco's North Beach in 1965, he didn't just come away knowing he'd heard some superior tunes. He also experienced a spiritual transformation, or a "baptism of sound," he later told the *San Francisco Weekly*.

In fact, King's newfound enlightenment was similar to the

experience of Coltrane himself, who had kicked a heroin habit and then told of his own religious awakening in 1957 on the liner notes to his *Love Supreme* album. "At that time, in gratitude, I humbly asked to be given the means and privilege to make others happy through music," Coltrane wrote.

Much the same can be said of King, who two years after Coltrane's death in 1967 founded a most unusual religious group called the St. John Will-I-Am Coltrane African Orthodox Church. It's known here simply as the Church of Coltrane, and it's the only church in the world that features Coltrane's music as the main theme of its liturgy.

One thing you can say about this church's services—they are never dull. They sometimes begin with jam sessions lead by King on the tenor saxophone. These free-flowing musical interludes sometimes last more than an hour. Those in the congregation also bring instruments to play or simply sing along. There are also biblical readings and sermons.

Since its founding, the church has taken an active role in providing food, clothing, and shelter for the needy. Then it became needy itself. Rising rents forced the church out of its longtime home in 2000. They've since found a temporary space at 930 Gough Street, where they hold regular Sunday services at 11:45 a.m. Call (415) 673-3572 for more information.

This Forecast Is Never Wrong

The Tonga Room and Hurricane Bar has the most predictable weather pattern of any place on the planet. For most of the time it's dry and comfortable, with moderate temperatures and no wind—what you'd expect from a large indoor room—except that every thirty minutes, a violent and clamorous thunderstorm erupts and produces torrents of rain. The dramatic shift in weather happens here like clockwork, because timers and machines control it all.

The indoor storm is the major attraction of this Polynesian-themed watering hole that also features tables with thatched roof coverings,

★ ★

a central lagoon, and a floating stage. There's an untraditional happy hour buffet featuring such Pacific Rim fare as pot stickers, spare ribs, and pork buns. And of course you can order from an assortment of fruity rum concoctions that are served in tiki glasses with pineapple chunks and sweet cherries speared on drink stirrers topped with paper umbrellas. The mai tai was invented here, and it's a house specialty.

What makes the Tonga Room so special is that it's housed within the refined splendor of the Fairmont Hotel. The pairing is about as incongruous as, well, an indoor rainstorm. The Fairmont Hotel is a marble-lined palace that has housed royalty and U.S. presidents since it first opened on Nob Hill in 1907. You pass through the gold-leaf trappings of the hotel to get to the Tonga's tropical island of kitsch. Just as you adjust to the jarring shift in atmosphere, it starts to rain—indoors. Then you know it's time to order another mai tai.

Paradise at the Tonga Room can be found at 950 Mason Street. If you call (415) 772-5278, you just might hear the sound of a heavy rain falling in the background.

The Benefits of Going Nowhere

The idea of going in circles suggests a frazzled state of frustration and inertia. Nothing could be more disheartening than thinking you're going somewhere only to end up right back where you started. This nightmarish scenario has been given a positive spin by a growing movement of circle walkers led by the Rev. Lauren Artress of San Francisco's Grace Cathedral.

In the early 1990s Artress spearheaded efforts to revive the centuries-old tradition of walking labyrinths as a way of calming your mind. A common feature of medieval cathedrals, labyrinths are circular paths leading to a center and then back to the start that people traverse as a kind of spiritual journey, or at least to clear their heads and lift their mood. Artress visited a famous one at the thirteenth-century Cathedral of Our Lady of Chartres in France that had been

Here you are encouraged to go around in circles.

covered over by chairs and long forgotten. It became her mission to restore that labyrinth as well as initiate efforts to build them around the world.

In 1995 the first permanent labyrinth constructed in the Western Hemisphere in 600 years was built at Grace Cathedral. It's located outside the cathedral doors and made of terrazzo stone. A labyrinth of tapestry had been created a year earlier inside the cathedral.

Artress then began holding labyrinth workshops around the country to encourage others to be built. She spent a great deal of time countering the negative connotation of the word *labyrinth*, which most people associated with a perplexing pattern of pathways meant to confuse and make people lose their way, akin to a maze. How could that be enjoyable and spiritually fulfilling?

Artress countered that these labyrinths were different and intended as easy-to-follow routes in and out of a circle. By walking them you would feel energized, clear-headed, and more at peace.

Artress is hardly going in circles with her promotion efforts. They've led to hundreds of labyrinths being built around the country in diverse locations such as churches, prisons, hospitals, parks, and retirement homes. She's also founded an organization called Veriditas, considered the voice of the labyrinth movement, and written an explanatory book. The group offers unique products such as portable labyrinths that allow users to let their fingers do the walking.

For more information stroll over to her group's Web site (www .veriditas.net) or call (415) 561-2921.

Art with a Big Heart

You can call it a case of bovine envy. After Chicago launched the popular Cows on Parade in 1999—artistically decorated fiberglass cows displayed around town—other cities herded up to follow in Chicago's hoofprints. Suddenly there were artworks depicting animals and even utensils turning up as public art in cities around North America, from fiberglass moose in Toronto to 6-foot-tall forks in Grand Forks, North Dakota. Take that, Chicago.

San Francisco followed suit in 2004 by announcing, appropriately on Valentine's Day, the start of "Hearts in San Francisco," a plan to display dozens of 5-foot-tall fiberglass hearts throughout the city, each uniquely decorated by a different local artist. The body's blood pump was deemed a suitable icon because of the city's celebrated anthem, "I Left My Heart in San Francisco." The public art project may also explain what happens to hearts that get left behind—they get turned into fanciful pieces of public art.

By summer 2004 the artfully decorated hearts were everywhere,

Lots of hearts have been left around San Francisco.

and they were colorful, whimsical, and sometimes a bit weird. *Global Heart* by Kara Maria features globs of green and blue flattened over the heart shape, while *Wolf Heart* depicts a plaid-eared wolf with bloodshot eyes wearing a bright-red bib. One heart shape at Union Square has a practical side—it powers a wireless Internet connection provided by Intel.

The project was a fund-raising effort for San Francisco General Hospital, and all the hearts were sponsored by donors. Many were eventually sold at auction, although a handful remain on the streets, including a prominent one in Union Square Park.

★ ★

A Lovable Dive-Bomber

Summer 2009 will be fondly remembered in San Francisco as the season of Swoops, a tiny blackbird that alternately terrorized and amused pedestrians in the city's Financial District and ultimately earned international fame and admiration.

From a perch on a metal awning of the City National Bank building at Front and California Streets, Swoops made frequent aerial attacks on passersby. The bird, protecting its nearby nest, had a variety of offensive moves, including the rapid flyby and the hovering double peck.

At first the bird attacks caught people off guard. But when video footage of the bombarding bird was broadcast around the world, Swoops drew a crowd. At lunchtime workers gathered to watch Swoops go into attack mode, never growing bored with the spectacle.

People purposely walked into the bird's territory to invite an attack. It became a mark of distinction to be pecked at by Swoops. Some compared it to the excitement of a thrill ride.

By the end of summer Swoops and her fledglings had moved on, gone but not forgotten.

It's a Small Christmas World

It's not Christmas season in San Francisco until Len Connacher packs up a U-Haul with dozens of storage boxes and heads to the city's two downtown Hyatt hotels. Working with a dozen helpers, Connacher spends about a week setting up winter wonderlands in miniature in the lobbies of both hotels.

Connacher, of Castro Valley, owns the world's largest collection of small ceramic Christmas objects from Department 56, a Minnesota maker of the decorative items.

With more than 10,000 pieces to choose from, Connacher arranges the objects to create hundreds of tiny cheerful wintry scenes, from small villages to ski slopes to snowy mountaintops. And Santas—lots of Santas. The effect of the small-scale lighted sets is enchanting, drawing thousands of people annually to experience it.

Connacher began his collection in 1980 and has been creating his Snow Villages at the Hyatts since the mid-1990s around Christmas time. If you'd like a wee bit of yuletide cheer, head over to either the Hyatt Regency on the Embarcadero at 5 Embarcadero Center (415-788-1234) or the Grand Hyatt at Union Square at 345 Stockton Street (415-398-1234).

The Brawn behind a City's Beautiful Feature

This city's signature tune, "I left My Heart in San Francisco," speaks poetically of a place where "little cable cars climb halfway to the stars." What the song never explains is how those little cars make it up all those really big hills. It's a song about love, after all, not mechanical energy.

For a less romantic but more scientific tribute to this city's trademark transportation, you have to visit the Cable Car Museum. It's here that you'll learn more than you probably need to know about what powers those quaint cars up the city's steep inclines and around all those sharp turns. You'll get a good slice of history through exhibits of photographs and artifacts such as a vintage fare box, ticket puncher, and old tokens. You can even examine the world's oldest cable car—a Clay Street Hill Railroad Car Number 8 from 1873, the only surviving car from this line. This is also the year cable car service began in San Francisco.

The museum is housed in a working powerhouse, so you get to see the guts behind all the glory of the cable car system. You can

This museum has a lot of pull.

gaze out at impressive heavy machinery including motors, cables, and pulleys that drive the whole operation. All four cables that power the city's cars enter and leave through this building and are in constant motion at a rate of 9.5 miles per hour. Grips in the cars use a device that looks like a large pair of pliers to attach the car to the cable if they want to go forward. To stop, without getting too technical, they simply let go of the cable and then apply a brake.

Historical exhibits also explain that horses were once used to pull the cars in the system's early days. But they couldn't make it up the hills. They also left behind a dirty mess on the streets—not a very romantic picture.

Take a ride over to the museum at 1201 Mason Street. Just follow the cable line. It's open every day except New Year's Day, Easter,
Thanksgiving, and Christmas. Hours vary by season. For more information call (415) 474-1887 or visit www.cablecarmuseum.org.

A Small Park with Big History

Historians may point to the discovery of gold at Sutter's Mill on January 24, 1848, as the start of the California gold rush. But the real
beginning to the gold rush actually happened a few months later, in
May, when an exuberant Sam Brannan boldly talked up the discovery
to a gathering in San Francisco's Portsmouth Square. To further stir
up excitement, he waved around vials of gold.

California's first school was built in this tiny park,
which has lots of firsts to boast about.

Brannan's display ignited gold fever in San Francisco, and thousands fled to the hills with dreams of instant riches.

With such a pivotal role in California's gold rush, Portsmouth Square is a noteworthy destination. But there's more. The tiny Chinatown park, bordered by Walter Lum Place and Kearny, Clay, and Washington Streets, is a veritable historical playground of many firsts.

The state's first public school was built here in 1847. The square was also the eastern end of the world's first cable car line, also opened in 1847.

The square got its name from another historical event, this one in 1846, when the United States was at war with Mexico. On July 9, John Montgomery, commander of the USS *Portsmouth,* went ashore to the square and first raised the American flag in San Francisco. The square was appropriately named for his ship.

Statues and historic plaques abound in the park, which today is a hub of activity that centers around a pagoda-themed children's playground, chess players, and groups engaged in tai chi exercises. There's even a statue of Robert Louis Stevenson to commemorate his stay in the city in 1879, when he made trips to the park to meet with sailors and gather research for his adventure novels.

"Whoa! Stop That Check!"

As corporate symbols go, the Wells Fargo stagecoach is pretty nifty, with rugged drivers urging on teams of hard-charging horses blazing trails across the Wild West. That seems like an exciting place to park your money.

The Wells Fargo History Museum in San Francisco, on the site where Henry Wells and William Fargo first opened for business in 1852, tells a less-glamorous side to the famed Fargo stagecoach. Exhibits here point out that the coaches traveled only 5 miles per hour.

The stagecoach journey could be a grueling experience. Coaches would seat up to eighteen passengers, with the nine people crammed inside granted only "nine inches of seat." Meals on some days could be black beans and coffee served from dirty tin cans.

One passenger is quoted in the exhibit calling the stagecoach journey "a continuous succession of unmitigated jolts."

People who long for the "good old days" may be jolted to reality by the information presented here. Better to look back with fondness and be grateful for what we have today—like ATM machines.

If you want a lesson on how things have improved since the days of the Old West, you can sit at an interactive exhibit on the telegraph machine and painstakingly send a message in Morse code to another

The stage is set for this vintage stage.

visitor sitting a few feet away. You'll walk away ever so thankful for modern means of speedier communication.

The museum's showpiece is an 1852 stagecoach that was in use until 1912. Also on display are three of the company's famed "treasure boxes," made of ponderosa pine and oak ribbon. They were used from 1862 to 1906 to transport money and other valuables. The exhibit points out that the arrival of the Wells Fargo stage was a welcome sight to California miners, since it meant they were getting paid. But the stage was also a prime target for highway robbers, and the best of them, including Black Bart, are given their due here in a comprehensive display. You are also invited to play amateur sleuth and follow clues to help solve one robbery case.

You won't have to hit any cash machine before visiting the museum at 420 Montgomery Street, since it's all free. The museum is open Monday through Friday from 9:00 a.m. to 5:00 p.m. Visit www. wellsfargohistory.com for more information.

Forget Its Name, Just Take Its Picture

More so than any other building in the city, the Transamerica Pyramid defines the San Francisco skyline. The city's tallest skyscraper, the Pyramid's unusual sleek design calls attention to itself and lets you know exactly where you are. It can only be San Francisco.

While the Pyramid is clear on its geography, it does have an identity problem. For one, the Transamerica Pyramid is no longer owned by Transamerica; it's owned by Aegon, a Dutch company. That hasn't stopped Transamerica, a financial and insurance service company, from using the building as its official logo.

And there's the "pyramid" part of the name. The Pyramid is not really a pyramid. The most appropriate design term would be obelisk, referring to a building shape with four sides and a pyramid on top.

But Aegon Obelisk? That just wouldn't do.

The Pyramid went up in 1972 and immediately became the tallest building west of the Mississippi, a title it held for a scant three years

Not all the great pyramids are in Egypt.

until a taller structure was erected in Los Angeles. The Pyramid is 853 feet tall and is mostly made of crushed quartz, which gives it its distinctive white appearance.

Its aerodynamic design, featuring two side wings, actually makes it look like some kind of rocket ship capable of lifting off into the air. But rooted it is at 600 Montgomery Street. The building houses office and retail space and is closed to the public—an unfortunate security precaution, since it does offer amazing views from inside.

The Pyramid is visible from many points around the city and is easily the most photographed building in San Francisco, one that is often featured in movies and commercials, including *View to a Kill and The Presidio.*

No matter what you call it, it sure is beautiful to look at.

Portals to an Illicit Past

San Franciscans have always exhibited a rebellious nature, and it was no different when the federal government imposed Prohibition on the nation from 1920 until 1933. Citizens here weren't going to let something like a constitutional amendment separate them from their favorite alcoholic beverages. Everyone just had to be more discreet about his or her drinking habits.

Historians have pointed out that San Francisco was a haven for speakeasies, with hundreds of clandestine drinking and gambling clubs set up around the city behind secret passageways and doors. Admission was usually via password, and patrons were asked to place their orders in hushed tones, or to "speak easy."

As a nod to this raucous period of adult entertainment in the city, new clubs have cropped up that re-create the speakeasy atmosphere and culture, albeit with modern touches such as DJs and more-sophisticated libations such as cucumber gimlets.

The Bourbon & Branch at 501 Jones Street (415-346-1735; www .bourbonandbranch.com), for example, requires customers to know a password for entrance, obtained by making reservations online. The password rotates daily and is computer generated from a long list of authentic Prohibition-era passwords. It's open Monday through Saturday from 6:00 p.m. until 2:00 a.m.

The Slide lounge elevates a simple piece of playground equipment to a whole other level. The bar, at 430 Mason Street (415-421-1916; www.slidesf.com), is located in a building that during Prohibition had a theater at the main level and a clandestine saloon underground. The bar was accessed by sliding down a chute.

The speakeasy's modern incarnation has its own version of the slide—a serpentine, custom-made mahogany slide that drops customers into the bar. It's recommended for patrons wearing pants, as the descent is rapid and can ruffle up those outfitted in skirts and dresses. For the less adventurous, stairs are an option. The lounge is open evenings Wednesday through Sunday.

A Head of State, All in His Head

With his feathered cap, military jacket with epaulettes, and a long saber at his side, Joshua Norton certainly projected the image of an important world figure. In fact he was America's first emperor. At least that's what he called himself, or rather decreed. Norton was a San Francisco businessman who had lost his fortune in the rice market. One day in 1859 he walked into a newspaper office and brightened up a slow news day by handing the editor a proclamation declaring himself to be Norton I, Emperor of the United States and Protector of Mexico.

The proclamation was duly published, and so began Emperor Norton's reign, certainly one of the more colorful personal histories in a city full of eccentric characters. For the next thirty years Norton issued decrees and paraded around San Francisco. He saluted people and was saluted back. He issued his own currency that was honored, with a wink, by local merchants. He dined for free at all city restaurants and wrote letters to Washington offering to mediate in the Civil War. At every theater opening in town, three seats were left open for Norton and his dogs.

He could be grand in his decrees, or sometimes base and prosaic. He issued proclamations to dissolve the United States Congress, while also declaring that a local hotel should give him a free room or else be banished.

Norton's decrees were popular reading, and the publication of them was good business for local newspapers—so much so that editors sometimes wrote their own to help sell papers.

Historians say that Norton was a beloved local figure who might not have been so crazy after all. He decreed in 1872 that a suspension bridge should be built connecting Oakland to San Francisco, several decades before the real one was constructed. When Norton died in 1880, thousands attended his funeral. They say he died penniless, but of course he had plenty of currency in the name of Norton I.

Very Soon You Will Read about Fortune Cookies

If your fate came wrapped in a cookie, would you take it to heart? Apparently yes, judging by the enduring popularity of the fortune cookie. The first fortune cookie was most likely introduced in San Francisco around 1920, making it an American invention, although it may have been inspired by the fourteenth-century tradition of Chinese soldiers passing secret messages hidden inside cakes.

The idea of offering destiny in a dessert has been a sweet success, with greater demand forcing most cookie companies to automate their operations to step up production in the twenty-first century. There are still a few shops that make the cookies by hand, and one of those is the Golden Gate Fortune Cookie Company, an out-of-the-way location in a cluttered alleyway in Chinatown. You can peer into the cramped factory space and watch two women seated before contraptions with moving conveyer belts containing horseshoe-shaped baking tins. The tins are pulled through ovens that bake the cookie dough. The women pull the round pancakes from the hot press and then, in a deft move, slip the slivers of paper with the fated messages into the flattened dough and give it a pinch to mold it into the

Here is where your fate is sealed.

fortune cookie's familiar shape. Operators here say they can produce up to 1,000 cookies an hour this way, but the pace seems a little slower at times. Watching the process may demystify the cookie's allure. You'll come away knowing that it was a human hand that sealed your fate and not some supernatural process. Of course you can also come away with a bag of either chocolate or vanilla cookies.

The company provides the rare opportunity to customize your own fortune. Or you can leave your fate in someone else's hands. See your destiny being folded at 56 Ross Alley.

A Monumental Gift to the City

She was born Charlotte Mignon Crabtree, but when she rose to prominence in the 1860s as San Francisco's most beloved entertainer, she was known simply as "Lotta." She could dance, sing, strum the banjo, and act. For several years her mother hauled Lotta's accumulating wealth around in a steamer trunk, but then she wisely invested it in real estate.

Even though Lotta eventually moved to the East Coast, she never forgot the city that helped launch her career. Lotta presented San Francisco with the gift of a gold-tinted iron fountain in 1875, one with ornamental flourishes and spitting lion heads.

Erected at the corner of Market and Kearny Streets, the fountain played a pivotal role in the city's recovery process after the devastating earthquake and fire of 1906. The fountain served as a meeting spot and place for survivors to exchange messages.

Ever since, survivors have gathered in the early-morning chill at the base of Lotta's Fountain to commemorate the quake's anniversary. It's an event that combines somber recollection with elements of frivolity. One longstanding tradition is the serving of free Bloody Marys, sometimes dispensed from an old fire truck. Kazoo playing is also involved.

The annual event, which begins at 5:00 a.m. every April 18 to mark the quake that struck exactly at 5:12 a.m. in 1906, is still held, even though the number of remaining survivors has dwindled considerably.

Lotta's Fountain, the city's oldest monument, was refurbished at a steep cost in 1998, reflecting the city's strong commitment to the fountain. It's an important symbol of the city's recovery from the 1906 quake—and a golden tribute to a gold rush–era entertainer who long ago captured the hearts of the city's residents.

A gold rush–era entertainer showered
the city with a whole lotta love.

The Heavenly Goddess Is on the Third Floor

When Chinese immigrants in San Francisco decided to found a temple in the mid-nineteenth century, it's no wonder they chose to honor the deity Tien Hau, the goddess of heaven and the sea. Many Chinese had endured a treacherous ocean journey to arrive safely in the Bay Area, so a tribute to Tien Hau was an obvious choice.

Built in 1852, the Tien Hau Temple is the oldest Chinese temple in the United States. To get there you climb three flights of stairs in a building in the heart of Chinatown, the smell of burning incense guiding you toward the destination on the top floor. You then enter

Some fresh fruit goes a long way at this historic temple.

the temple, a small quiet room with a balcony. The space is decorated with a densely packed display of red lanterns hanging from the ceiling and richly adorned gold tapestries.

Visitors to this Taoist temple are invited to make offerings of food, drink, and incense in the hope of being granted good fortune for themselves, loved ones, and even for the souls of people no longer living.

The room is awash in red and gold and features several colorful altars that contain offerings to the gods. Most prominent are vases of flowers and bowls containing oranges, apples, and persimmons.

Temple officials say that Tien Hau was born a mere mortal in 960 and was imbued in her lifetime with the power to summon wind and rain to ease people's sufferings. Following her death at age twenty-eight, people began worshipping her as a goddess who aids people in trouble, in particular those at sea.

The temple is located at 125 Waverly Place and is open daily from 10:00 a.m. until 4:00 p.m.

Something's Fishy about This Fish Store

The sign outside says this is an aquarium store, and sure enough, inside you'll find familiar looking aquarium tanks filled with water. But if you come here expecting to see lots of fish, you'll get a dose of cold water splashed on those expectations.

The focus at Aqua Forest Aquarium is not on fish but on the aquarium decor that fish swim around. AFA is the first nature aquarium store in the United States, playing upon a trend that began in Japan and is now spreading around the world.

This store goes way beyond the typical aquarium decorations of years past, which may have included a few plastic rocks and fake plants. The nature aquarium movement emphasizes wondrous landscapes of living underwater vegetation that would be the envy of any self-respecting gardener out of water. Plant branches shoot out of the tank tops here, evidence of the robust health of the assorted vegetation.

★ ★

It's a complex task to keep everything healthy and vital, according to owner Steven Lo, as it requires special tank pumps and careful attention to the soil, lights, and filtration. When it works, as it does throughout this store, the results can be extraordinary.

"It's more like living art," Lo says. The development of nature aquariums, Lo points out, grew from the Japanese tradition of flower

Steven Lo, underwater landscape artist

arranging. A lot of thought goes into composition, depth of field, and colors. Making it work underwater is quite a challenge.

The store boasts all the supplies needed to get you going at home, including aquatic plants from all over the world, various equipment, and even freshwater tropical fish. Visitors, Lo says, "get inspired and then they want to have a tank." When they commit, the store is there to provide guidance and all the needed materials.

Drop by and have a look at 1718 Fillmore Street. The store is closed on Tuesday but open the rest of the week from 11:00 a.m. to 7:00 p.m. and on Sunday from noon until 6:00 p.m. Call (415) 929-8883 for more information, or visit them on the Web at www.aqua-forestaquarium.com.

A Real Double Take

There's no official award for the world's most charismatic identical twins, but if there were, it would surely go to Nob Hill sisters Marian and Vivian Brown. The vivacious elderly pair (they're coy about their age, although their rumored birth year is 1927) enjoy parading around the city in identical snappy outfits to go with their identically coiffed hair, matching lipstick, and, well, you get the picture. Aside from a brief experimentation with independence early in their youth, they've dressed exactly alike their whole lives. They have more than a hundred outfits to choose from daily and are often spotted walking about on their way to a meal.

The sisters arrived in the city in 1970 to begin secretarial jobs and retired in 1993 to start their real careers, as ambassadors for the city's quirky side. They've made cameo appearances in films and commercials and are probably included in more travel photo albums than any other San Franciscans, as they are stopped dozens of times each day with photo requests.

If you'd like to snap a shot, some of their favorite haunts include the Nob Hill Cafe, the Fog City Diner, and Uncle Vito's.

A Moving Experience for Your Ears

With its brown-paneled storefront exterior, the Audium looks pretty plain from the outside. But step inside this unique theater of "sound sculpted space" and the performance you'll enjoy will be anything but ordinary.

You'll walk into a small foyer sparsely decorated with strange sculptures and paintings. Sounds such as the amplified noise of water dripping and a mechanized hum play in the background. The offered refreshment is instant coffee served in Styrofoam cups. But this is just a prelude to what amounts to a trippy, science fiction form of entertainment.

The main show takes place in a forty-nine-seat theater filled with chairs placed in a circle. The room is outfitted with 174 speakers placed all around. The lights are turned down and a man steps onto a raised platform. He then entertains the audience for the next hour with a performance of "sculpted sound"—a concert of various noises that include instruments, voices, and electronic noises and sound effects.

When Sam Shaff began offering these sound performances in the 1960s, he knew he was ahead of his time. But now mainstream sound engineers have caught up with him, as both home and commercial theaters are designed more for effects like surround sound and moving sound.

"It's like conducting an orchestra," Shaff says. "You have to, in effect, learn how to orchestrate for various types of instruments, where space is one of those instruments and so are the speakers."

Shaff composes and records these sound compositions, but each performance is different, depending on how he decides to move that sound around in the performance hall on any given night. "I move the sound and place it and give it energy. I also play the color characteristics of the speakers," he says.

Pretty impressive, considering that Shaff operates in the dark and must move controls on an unlit sound board.

After the show, visitors can wander back into the foyer where Shaff is waiting. He debriefs the audience, giving everyone an overview of his longtime work in sound, and then takes questions. If you want to listen in, make a reservation for a weekend performance at 1616 Bush Street by calling (415) 771-1616.

These Dogs Really Had Their Day

In 1862 the city of San Francisco passed a law banning all dogs without a muzzle or leash in downtown, a law designed to remedy the problem of stray canines.

The law notably didn't apply to two stray mutts known as Bummer and Lazarus. The dogs, known for the ability to catch rats and their mutual devotion, were given a pass because they were celebrity canines to an extraordinary degree. Newspaper reporters had been covering their every exploit, be it stealing bones from other dogs or killing a prodigious number of rats in a day. So the public wouldn't stand for any harm coming to Bummer or Lazarus, even though they were in violation of the law.

Their exploits were of mythic proportion. Newspapers reported that the dogs first met when Bummer rescued Lazarus from a bad fight with another dog and nursed him back to health and that they were devoted to each other after this initial bonding. Lazarus died in 1863 and Bummer two years later. Both mutts received lengthy obituaries in the press.

A plaque dedicated to Bummer and Lazarus is located outside the Transamerica Pyramid and tells the story of two dogs who were above the law and headliners of their day.

Feel Like a Cowboy, Without Ever Getting on a Horse

Probably no other pants evoke the spirit of the American West like blue jeans, denim trousers invented in San Francisco by Levi Strauss and Jacob Davis. Climb into a pair of jeans and you immediately feel more rugged and pioneering. Rebellious even. And comfortable of course.

Strauss, a Bavarian immigrant, arrived in San Francisco in 1853 to open a dry goods business. Looking to capitalize on the booming economy fueled by the gold rush, he instead found his fortune in denim. Davis, a tailor, showed Strauss his clever way of using rivets to make denim work clothes more resilient. In 1873 they patented this rivet system for making "waist overalls," and blue jeans were born.

One of the most interesting tidbits of this history is that Strauss's first name, now synonymous with jeans, originally was Loeb, which would be a funny name to call jeans, as in: "It's a casual party, right? I'll just put on my Loebs." Thankfully Strauss had changed his first name by the time he arrived in America.

Jeans were a hit with workers and eventually went mainstream in the early twentieth century, popularized by the many Levi's-clad cowboys appearing in Westerns. The rest is apparel history, as Levi jeans remain an enduring American symbol, much more than just pants.

You can explore some of that history at the company's visitor center, which houses exhibits and company archives, including the most expensive pair of jeans on the planet. That's a pair of denim pants made by the company in 1879 and originally sold for 75 cents. When the pants turned up at an auction in 2001, the company bought them back for more than $46,000. The historic pants are stored in a vault, but other vintage Levi clothing is on display here, including a pair of 501 pants from 1890, Aloha shirts from the 1940s, and tailored men's shirts from the 1930s.

You can also sit in a small theater and watch five decades of Levi broadcast commercials, from the 1960s to the present, and study the company's evolving marketing strategy, from touting the clothing's ruggedness to promoting its sex appeal.

The visitor center at 1155 Battery Street is open 9:00 a.m. to 6:00 p.m. Monday through Friday and 10:00 a.m. to 5:00 p.m. on weekends. Call (415) 501-6000 for additional information.

2

North Bay

San Francisco's Old *Ship Ale House is a cool name for an urban pub, but its origin is more historical than creative. You see, this San Francisco hangout really is an old ship. It was grounded during the gold rush days and then turned into a saloon that served ale.*

There's plenty of history in this section of the city, with some of it hiding in plain sight, like the Old Ship Ale House. Television was invented in a Green Street laboratory, although you have to search for the marker that commemorates this monumental invention. You can also find some of the oldest dough in the world here—and taste it too—at Boudin's on Fisherman's Wharf. There's a museum dedicated to the Beat Generation, and a military pet cemetery located in the Presidio, which has a long history as a military base, although it's now a prime recreation area.

Here you can also find the city's last remaining eight-sided house, a relic from a nineteenth-century fad when octagon homes were more in vogue. And there's an eyeful of history at the Museum of Vision, the country's only exhibit hall devoted to ophthalmology.

You can experience history here in a real hands-on way. At the Musee Mecanique at Pier 45, you don't just admire antique coin-operated games but actually play them. After that, stroll a short distance and set sail on a World War II liberty ship, the only one of its kind still capable of hitting the high seas.

The Image Maker

You may know that Alexander Graham Bell invented the telephone and Thomas Edison the lightbulb. But do you know who invented television?

That would be Philo Farnsworth. And he did it in San Francisco.

Farnsworth was only twenty-one years old when he electronically transmitted the first television picture in a small loft laboratory at 202 Green Street on September 7, 1927. It wasn't much of a show. Using his "Image Dissector" he broadcast the moving image of a

The road to *American Idol* started here.

straight line etched on a glass slide to a receiver in another room. His reported response was decidedly low key: "There you have it— electronic television."

Even with such a world-changing invention to his credit, Farnsworth remains an obscure historical figure, partly because of a protracted patent battle he waged with RCA over invention rights—a case he eventually won.

Farnsworth cared little for what became of his invention, even preventing his own son from watching any programs. Bad television shows can do that to a person. When he appeared in 1957 on the game show *I've Got a Secret,* he said of his invention, "Sometimes it's most painful." But he later added, "I think generally speaking it has been a blessing."

The building that contained his laboratory still stands, today housing several offices. Outside you'll find a nondescript plaque mounted on a plain concrete slab. Shadowed by an overhanging tree branch, the plaque commemorates the day the "Genius of Green Street" invented television.

A Burning Controversy Engulfs a Familiar Landmark

Coit Tower is a clearly visible and easily recognized city sight perched atop Telegraph Hill. Not so clear is the intent of the architect who designed it.

When it was dedicated in 1933, the 210-foot tower struck many San Franciscans as looking like a giant fire hose nozzle. That would be fitting enough, since the late Lillie Hitchcock Coit donated the funds to build it. Coit was a wealthy financier's wife and a life-long supporter of the San Francisco Fire Department, especially her beloved Knickerbocker Engine Company No. 5.

As a kid she had stopped on her way home from school to help the engine company put out a blaze, and she maintained a lifelong fascination with the dashing firefighters and their snazzy uniforms. She often hung out as one of the guys, playing cards and smoking cigars, and visited them in the hospital if they were injured. She was voted an honorary member of the Knickerbocker crew in 1863. Some have even suggested that the tower's cylindrical shape and tapered end were more of a tribute to her affection for the manhood of these gallant firemen.

Amid the snickers, architect Arthur Brown Jr. tried for years to douse rumors that his prized work was actually a re-creation of a fire hose nozzle. But the perception has been impossible to extinguish.

You can judge for yourself with a visit to 1 Telegraph Hill Boulevard. The tower also contains magnificent Works Progress Administration (WPA) murals. Call (415) 362-0808 for more information.

A Little Water Music

The sound of the sea can be music to the ears, which may explain why so many people flock to the beach on vacation. A unique San Francisco environmental sculpture known as the *Wave Organ* takes the musical capability of the ocean to its maximum degree.

Visitors to the *Wave Organ* need to hear some explanation before they can fully appreciate what they've come upon. The sculpture sits at the end of a jetty off Yacht Road, past the St. Francis Yacht Club, and looks at first glance like an unusual stone bench where can you sit and enjoy the spectacular views of the Golden Gate Bridge and San Francisco Bay.

But the organ is not so much for the eyes as for the ears.

Artist Peter Richards created the sculpture in 1986 with help from stonemason George Gonzalez. What's visible on the surface are stone and marble sitting areas that feature fluted concrete pipes placed all around. These twenty-five pipes actually run all the way under the water and are designed to capture and amplify the various sounds of the waves and the movement of the tides in and out.

Visitors can place their ears up to the ends of the pipes and listen to the music of the waves, which turns out to be an assortment of gurgles, sloshes, and rumblings.

Here's where the ocean gives a concert.

True, it's not like a concert in the traditional sense, but the *Wave Organ* provides a decidedly unique listening experience. Visitors are advised to come when the tide is high, when the sounds are most noticeable.

The *Wave Organ's* instrumentation is composed of PVC pipe and cement; the seating areas are constructed from stone salvaged from the Laurel Hill Cemetery—a gold rush-era graveyard that was demolished in 1950. So you can sit on a piece of history, enjoy the views, and listen to a subtle symphony of the sea.

In Ship Shape, but Not a Ship

When the gold rush hit, hundreds of sailors abandoned their ships and headed for the hills in search of instant riches. This sudden exodus led to some creative recycling efforts of the abandoned vessels.

The sailing ship *Arkansas*, for example, was turned into a saloon when an innovative businessman carved a hole in its hull and connected the ship to a nearby pier with a gangplank. Originally called the Old Ship Ale House, it's now a pub located at 298 Pacific Street.

The grounded *Euphemia* was transformed into the city's first prison in 1850, while a hotel was built on the remains of the partly burned *Niantic*.

The gold rush was certainly a boom for creative construction. Other abandoned gold rush ships were turned into office buildings, warehouses, and even a church.

This is one saloon that's really grounded.

★ ★

And the Beats Go On

If Jack Kerouac, Allen Ginsberg, and Neal Cassady were the face of the Beat Generation, then North Beach was its place. In the late 1950s and early 1960s, this San Francisco neighborhood was crammed with deep-thinking poets and writers furiously putting down rebellious words on paper.

Some of the history remains here, most notably in the form of the city's venerable literary bookstore City Lights (415-362-8193), located at 261 Columbus Avenue.

It was City Lights founder Lawrence Ferlinghetti who published

Beat a path to this museum.

Ginsburg's seminal work "Howl," which drew howls of protest from some that it was obscene, a charge that Ferlinghetti helped defend against successfully in 1957.

With all the Beat history looming behind every storefront here, it's no wonder that a museum dedicated to the literary movement opened up. The Beat Museum is a bit like a Beat poem itself: free-flowing, provocative, and somewhat ambiguous.

The two-story exhibit space sets out to explain and chronicle this decidedly American literary movement with historical photographs, press clippings, memorabilia, and of course books. There are several vintage books, including foreign editions of Jack Kerouac's *On the Road* and a signed copy of Ginsburg's "Howl." While it wasn't Kerouac's greatest literary work, there's even a check for $10.08 made out to a liquor store with his signature.

These artifacts make sense here. But then there are items such as an old printing machine that appears to have no relation to any Beat literary work, other than it looks old. And upstairs, visitors encounter some worn pieces of furniture, which also have no connection to any specific Beat writer. They are just there to give people a sense of what it might have been like to live in a Beat-era pad.

One of the best things to do here is to view the continuously running video on the Beats, which includes gems such as a reading by Kerouac while accompanied on the piano by Steve Allen.

So dust off your beret and head over to the museum at 540 Broadway Street. It's open daily from 10:00 a.m. until 7:00 p.m. Call (800) 537-6822 or visit www.thebeatmuseum.org for more information.

Touch, but Don't Look

Fumbling in the dark in search of a light switch can be a frustrating and even frightening moment. Would you subject yourself to that experience for more than an hour, knowing that there was no light switch within reach to come to your rescue?

★ ★

That's the challenge presented by the Tactile Dome at the Exploratorium, an innovative science museum. The two-story Exploratorium, opened by physicist Dr. Frank Oppenheimer in 1969, is filled with pioneering hands-on exhibits meant to educate visitors about science and human perception.

Of all the exhibits here, the Tactile Dome stands out. It's a geodesic dome entered through a light-lock chamber that beckons visitors into a world of total darkness. Visitors spend seventy-five minutes crawling around inside, mostly using the only sense of any use in this darkened space: touch. What people can feel and sense are different materials, shapes, and textures, as well as varied temperatures. There are mazelike pathways of tubes and chutes to navigate through.

Some visitors find the dome exhilarating, while others call it harrowing. Richard Register, an artist who helped create the dome, says on the Exploratorium's Web site that the dome will summon up "vague fears of death, opening an inner perspective, a magic theater pouring through the mind from places unknown."

The goal here isn't to scare people of course but to make them appreciate the underutilized sense of touch.

If you're ready to enter this tiny world without light, feel your way over to the Exploratorium at 3601 Lyon Street. The dome is open Tuesday through Sunday, with the first group going in at 10:15 a.m. and the last at 5:00 p.m. On weekends there's an extra session at 6:45 p.m. Call (415) 561-0362 for reservations, and visit the museum's award-winning Web site (www.exploratorium.edu) for more information and lots of great online content.

The Military's Soft Underbelly

The Presidio served as a military outpost for three nations for more than 200 years before its conversion into park space in the early 1990s. The transformation into a prime recreation area has been so complete that it's hard to recognize that this sprawling area was once a military base. The Presidio served as an army post for first Spain,

Fallen, furry military heroes are honored here.

then Mexico, and finally the United States, which used it to house
Army families for more than 150 years, ending in 1989.

One of the most telling signs of the Presidio's military past is a tiny
plot of land in the shadow of Monterey pine trees that served for
many years as the base's pet cemetery.

Depending on their mood, visitors may find this spot either charm-
ing or spooky. There are more than one hundred grave markers paying tribute to the beloved pets of military families who once lived
here, from dogs and cats to lizards, mice, hamsters, parakeets, and
pigeons.

The grave markers range from basic wooden headstones with
painted words to more elaborate stone markers complete with photos and fancy engravings. To add to the cemetery's eerie atmosphere,

some of the markers have fallen into disrepair and are perched at odd angles.

But there is much warmth in the tributes, which include heartfelt messages for pets lost too soon and those who were sorely missed.

"My beloved and eternal friend," one marker reads. "Brought love and joy to so many," says another. Some cry out the names of their pets, such as "My Pet Whiskers," "Our Knucklehead Parakeet," or "Boris, the Russian Tortoise."

Although some pet graves date to the early 1900s, National Park Service officials say that the tradition of burying army pets here came into vogue during the 1950s, when there were more than 2,000 U.S. Army families on the base.

The cemetery is surrounded by a white picket fence near the bottom of a hill that overlooks the Golden Gate Bridge near the intersection of McDowell and Crissy Field Avenues. A construction project for an elevated road that passes over the cemetery once threatened its future, but park officials have said the cemetery will be preserved, so Whiskers and Boris and others can be assured an eternal rest.

The Mother of All Doughs

When you bite into a slice of San Francisco sourdough bread, the bread bites back. The city's signature loaf is no wimpy white bread.

The bread's distinctive sour taste, coupled with its crunchy golden crust and soft chewy center, has been a winning combination since the city's gold rush days. The bread was so popular with gold miners that they were nicknamed sourdoughs. Good thing for them they didn't favor pumpernickel.

The key ingredient to sourdough's sweet success is a wild yeast found only in San Francisco. No one is quite sure why, but it probably has something to do with the city's perpetual fog.

French baker Isidore Boudin first harvested the magical sourdough yeast in 1849 and then used it to make the seminal loaf.

Amazingly, Boudin's original starter dough has been continuously

This is where things go sour at Boudin's.

replenished and preserved as "mother dough." The venerable San Francisco bakery now churns out more than 10,000 fresh loaves daily, and each one contains a portion of Boudin's original yeast mixture.

The mother dough was almost toast during San Francisco's 1906 earthquake, but Louise Boudin rescued it and stashed it safely away in a bucket. A few generations later, the mother dough got star treatment when it was ceremoniously carted in a vintage wagon to Boudin's new flagship store at 160 Jefferson Street at Fisherman's Wharf.

★ ★

The site includes a demonstration kitchen that features a 300-foot-long observation window that's visible from the street. Visitors can peer in as bakers shape loaves by hand.

You can also chew on some San Francisco history here with a stop at Boudin's Sourdough Museum. This dough-themed exhibit space features vintage photos and artifacts that highlight the close relationship between sourdough bread and San Francisco's development from the gold rush to the present.

How to Stay Dry while Moving through Water

The best way to learn about sea creatures is to dive into the water and watch marine life unfold in its natural setting. That means scuba equipment and dive training and, let's face it, it's not for everyone. A painless and dry alternative to getting a diver's-eye view of

Go deep-sea diving with your clothes on.

underwater life is Pier 39's Aquarium of the Bay. Opened in 1996 and renovated in 2001, the aquarium offers a combination conveyer belt ride and underwater adventure. Here you dive into the water by taking a short elevator ride. Then you step onto a slow-moving walkway that pulls you through two acrylic tube tunnels where you are surrounded by more than 700,000 gallons of seawater teeming with hundreds of fish from the San Francisco Bay.

You won't feel like Jacques Cousteau or anything, but you won't need a mask and you'll be breathing through your own nostrils, not some air tube. The view is quite spectacular, and with so little effort on your part. You don't even have to walk. Everything from giant schools of silvery anchovies to flounder, bat rays, and sturgeons cruise by on every side as you constantly swivel your head to take in all the underwater scenery. There are even several varieties of sharks and a giant Pacific octopus lurking about.

It takes about thirty minutes to pass through the tunnel, unless you hop off the walkway occasionally to inspect something more closely, such as one of the many starfish stuck to the side of the acrylic tube.

You return to the surface by way of another elevator ride without a care about getting the bends. There you'll find some touch pools where you can pet leopard sharks and bat rays. Then you make a final stop at a gift shop, certainly not a typical end to most scuba dives. For more information contact the aquarium at (415) 623-5353 or visit http://aquariumofthebay.org.

A Very Spooky Store

The International Spy Shop doesn't hide its whereabouts. There's nothing clandestine about its location along a busy street at Fisherman's Wharf that features a giant sign proclaiming its identity. You don't need an overcoat or a secret password to enter.

Here everyone is welcome to come in from the cold and explore the world of surveillance, eavesdropping, personal protection, and assorted spying activities.

There's no secret about what's inside this store.

On one level, this is a serious business—the shop caters to security professionals craving the latest in spy equipment. On another level, it's a great place to explore for those people with a more casual interest in spying who want to immerse themselves in a room full of cool James Bond gadgets.

Take, for example, stylish-looking watches that also double as recording devices. Or eyeglasses with hidden cameras, hidden wall safes, secret microphones, and assorted listening devices—even lawn sprinkler heads that can be used to hide valuables. There are posters from famous spy movies on sale, as well as a classic black T-shirt emblazoned with the slogan "I Was Not Here."

Lest anyone think spying is all fun and games, the store offers serious weaponry, including guns, knives, and mini hatchets, and an assortment of personal-protection items such as pepper spray, handcuffs, batons, and stun guns.

Walking around all this surveillance equipment is bound to make anyone feel paranoid, a suspicion that's confirmed as visitors view their video images on several monitors around the store. Yes, you are being followed, and it's all caught on tape.

Follow the trail to 555 Beach Street from 11:00 a.m. to 7:00 p.m. Sunday through Thursday and from 10:00 a.m. to 10:00 p.m. on Friday and Saturday. For a kick you can dial (888) 775-ISPY (4775) or visit them on the Web at www.internationalspyshop.com.

Eight Is Enough

Four sides to a house may seem like plenty to some, and if you want to get fancy, maybe six.

Around the mid-nineteenth century, however, some people believed that a house should have eight sides.

Popularized by a book called, appropriately enough, *The Octagon House,* this unusual home design was a reaction to a darker Victorian style. Houses with eight sides were built to allow more light to enter. And it sure gave a home unique curb appeal.

Several octagon houses were built in San Francisco, and one of them remains. Dating to 1861, the city's Octagon House has been restored under the guidance of the National Society of the Colonial Dames of America, a historical society. The house is open a few hours each month for public viewing, if stepping inside a house with eight sides has always been your goal.

Enter this quirky dwelling and you're likely to take the side of the eight-sided house people. There's definitely something cheery, even playful, about a house with so many sides. It certainly offers decorating options not available to those who live in more traditional homes.

The bonus here is that the local Colonial Dames chapter has outfitted the house with many of its historical treasures, including furniture, portraits, rugs, and silver from the Federal and colonial periods.

In addition, in an upstairs room there's a display of letters and documents featuring the signatures of fifty-four of the fifty-six signers

★ ★

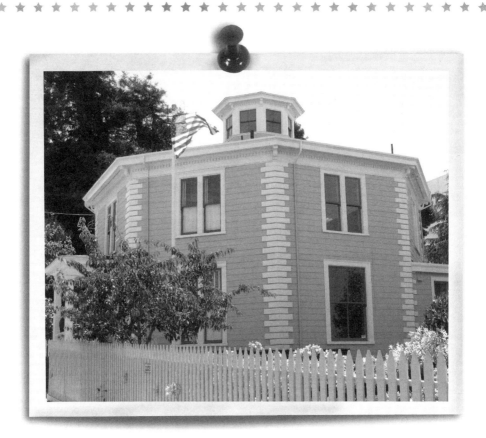

Eight-sided homes were once a popular choice.

of the Declaration of Independence. There's also a Queen Anne–style card table featuring cards set up to play a game called Lanterloo, popular in late-eighteenth-century America.

In keeping with the house's whimsical nature, there's a chest of drawers upstairs that includes a secret pull-out compartment where owners would have hidden their valuables.

The Octagon House is open for viewing at 2645 Gough Street on the second Sunday and the second and fourth Thursdays of every month, except during holidays and the month of January, from noon to 3:00 p.m. Call (415) 441-7512 for more information.

Come on in, the Water's . . . Frigid

The federal prison at Alcatraz was considered escape-proof because it was surrounded by the icy waters of San Francisco Bay. Inmates just didn't think a chilly swim was worth a shot at freedom. Which can only make you marvel at the many San Franciscans who every day freely plunge into the bay for recreation. The city has a long-standing tradition of cold-water swimming centered around two organizations located at Aquatic Park: the Dolphin Club and the South End Rowing Club.

Head to Aquatic Park near the intersection of Jefferson and Hyde Streets and you're bound to see a few club members merrily swimming away near a line of buoys set parallel to the shore. Members have disdain for those who don wet suits. These folks prefer to plunge in equipped only with swimsuit, thermal cap, and a lot of nerve.

Perils abound of course, including hypothermia, smelly ocean scents, and nipping sea lions. But that hasn't deterred anyone at either club since they were founded in the 1870s.

In addition to daily informal swims, both clubs organize special swims throughout the year, including ones that go from Alcatraz to Aquatic Park, a distance of 1.5 miles in water that may be a bone-chilling 50 degrees. They also promote marathon swims and rowing events.

Some members emerge from their swims with a new appreciation for life and a desire to party. The motto of the South End Rowing Club is to "love life and enjoy good food and drink."

If a shivery swim sounds like your idea of fun, you're welcome to drop by and sign up for the day at either the Dolphin Club, at 502 Jefferson Street (415-441-9329), or the South End Rowing Club, at 500 Jefferson Street (415-776-7372). Or just bundle up and enjoy the scene from shore, happy to be dry and warm.

Squatting on the Dock of the Bay

Pier 39 officials were at first slow to react to the golden egg tossed in
their laps in the winter of 1989, when dozens of sea lions took over
a dock and refused to leave. Their misgivings probably had something
to do with the fact that these unwelcome guests stank, spewed nasty
fish breath, barked loudly day and night, and otherwise behaved in
uncivilized ways, as wild animals tend to do.

Then Pier 39 merchants noticed that the smelly intruders were
attracting attention and, more important, tourist dollars. So they had
a change of heart. After all, what's a measly old dock if it means a

Pier 39's entertainers often sleep on the job.

serious uptick in business? What's evolved since is a win-win situation: The sea lions have a snazzy place with a good food supply where they can haul out for the winter, and the pier's restaurants and shops get a major tourist attraction that doesn't require a union contract.

About 900 sea lions now winter on the pier's D dock doing what sea lions do, which isn't much. Activities include napping, cuddling, yelping, and shoving each other around during playful displays of dominance. This limited repertoire has scored big with the public. Visitors have flocked here ever since word of the sea lion invasion got out. Pier 39 officials could not have planned it any better, since the sea lion population peaks during the normal low of the tourist season. It's no wonder that the pier has erected a statue in honor of the sea lions and also renamed an access path Sea Lion Way.

Now there are bleacher seats set up for people to watch the action. While most of the sea lions seem oblivious to the throngs, a few hams play up to the crowd, waddling around noisily on a platform only a few feet away from everyone. Some have settled in so nicely that they no longer migrate south during summer. Although most leave after winter, a few dozen now stay on permanently, providing the pier with a year-round tourist magnet. For all that, putting up with their stinky breath is a small price to pay.

You've Really Got to See This Place

If you've misplaced your glasses, you might want to check with the folks at the Museum of Vision. After all, they've got more than 3,000 pairs on hand.

Of course the museum's collection of spectacles is more historic in nature, which fits with its mission to be an education resource for medical professionals and the general public.

Yes, the entire history of eye care is documented here with the museum's more than 38,000 artifacts, which include rare books, documents, photographs, and medical equipment and instruments

**The Museum of Vision lets you see
about the history of eye care.**

related to the field of ophthalmology. The museum is the only one in the United States devoted to preserving the history of ophthalmology.

The museum's collection dates to the third century BC and includes exhibits on some of the earliest attempts at cataract surgery more than 2,000 years ago. The procedure called for the use of needles to push back a cloudy lens to clear up vision.

Also on display are many sets of eyewash cups, once-popular items used to help keep eyes clean from pollution. In this exhibit you can find many of the ornamental eyewash cups and the various eyewash products that were in vogue in the early twentieth century.

The museum is often used by medical researchers and historians, who dig into the archives here to explore the rich history of eye and vision treatment. The museum is located at 655 Beach Street, in the headquarters of the Foundation of the American Academy of Ophthalmology.

The general public is welcome here too. There's plenty here to see for even those with a casual interest in vision, including exhibits on common eye diseases, unusual spectacles from around the world, and vintage ophthalmology equipment dating back hundreds of years. You can make an appointment to visit from 9:00 a.m. to 5:00 p.m. on Monday through Friday by calling (415) 561-8502.

Filling Up a Big Slot in His Life

When Edward Zelinsky was eleven he won five quarts of oil during a drawing at a local theater, a prize that didn't interest him much. So he sold the oil and used the proceeds to buy his first penny arcade game, fueling a lifelong passion for collecting coin-operated wonders. By the time he was an adult, Zelinsky had amassed the world's largest private collection of mechanical art. He owns more than 300 items that include antique slot machines, automated musical instruments and players, and coin-operated amusements such as mechanical fortune-tellers, peep shows, dioramas, and games.

Zelinsky shared his collection with the public by opening one of San Francisco's more unusual attractions, the Musee Mecanique. Although it is labeled a museum, there is none of that stuffy, hands-off attitude here. Visitors can admire these ancient marvels and, if they have loose change, can play them as well. Everything displayed is in working order and comes to life when coins are inserted.

There are dioramas such as Royal Court, where tiny, elaborately designed figures dance in a miniature, ornate French-style ballroom. More sinister are animated scenes such as the French Guillotine, where doors of a castle swing open to reveal a depiction of a beheading, and the Opium Den, where staggering, skeleton-like figures portray the harrowing effects of narcotic consumption.

On the risqué side there are several peep shows such as Susie the can-can dancer and another automated viewer that offers people a chance to "see what the belly dancer does on her day off." These salacious come-ons promise more than they deliver.

The museum features several automated musical presentations, including a box with musical monkeys and a massive carnival show with one hundred different moving parts, including a Ferris wheel, children's plane ride, and acrobats in motion.

For more traditional arcade fare, you can appeal to mechanical fortune-tellers who spit out your fate on small cards or test your pucker power on the Kiss-o-meter, which offers ratings from ice-cold to hot stuff. Automated antique skill games include arm wrestling, hockey, and baseball.

It's all fun and games, with a big dose of cultural history too. The collection is up and working at Pier 45 at the end of Taylor Street at Fisherman's Wharf. For more information you can visit the museum's Web site at www.museemechanique.org or call (415) 346-2000.

The Short and Winding Road

You have to question the enduring appeal of a block of Lombard Street that's known as the Crookedest Street in the World. Never mind that "crookedest" really isn't a word. Even without the catchy title, this would be one of the most famous passageways on Earth.

The stretch of Lombard between Hyde and Leavenworth Streets is a twisted journey with more curves than a Hollywood sexpot. This maddening boulevard is the least practical of roads to travel, yet drivers just can't stay away. It consists of eight turns so radically sharp that "hairpin" hardly describes them. Cars become like slalom skiers in slow motion, shushing back and forth at a walking pace.

Despite its flaws, this is a road most traveled by, a rite of passage for tourists and coming-of-age locals with new driver's licenses. The traffic jams caused by cars waiting to make the coiling descent during peak tourist season have enraged nearby residents, and there are frequent calls to shut it down. City officials have responded by saying that if people want to drive themselves crazy by cruising Lombard, it's their legal

Lombard Street offers a thrill ride at 5 miles per hour.

right. The street has withstood every challenge to close it to traffic.

When the loony lane first opened in 1922, it wasn't intended to have the thrilling appeal of a roller-coaster attraction. The switch-backs were created to ease the ride down the steep hill. But that's all forgotten today.

In addition to driving Lombard, a popular tradition is to stand at the bottom and pose for a souvenir photograph with the picturesque and curvaceous street in the background. If you're driving down the hill, you'll see the crowd looking up at you. You can also glimpse spectacular views of the city and bay. But this is one time you'd better keep your eyes on the road—if you can keep up with its tortuous path.

If you want a similar thrill on a markedly less-crowded road, drive over to Vermont Street between Twenty-first and Twenty-second Streets. This stretch of road is just as windy, and hardly anyone heads to this part of town for the crooked road experience. At the top of the hill you'll find McKinley Park, a nice recreational area offering a grassy field, playground, walking trails, and nice views of the city.

Still at Liberty to Ship Out

If you want to learn what life was like on the high seas during World War II, you can read about it in a book. In San Francisco there's a better option: Climb aboard a fully functional World War II Merchant Marine vessel and experience it firsthand.

More than 2,700 so-called liberty ships were built and employed during the war, and almost all were later mothballed and dismantled. The SS *Jeremiah O'Brien* is the only remaining liberty ship in its original condition that is fully functional. Not only can you climb aboard but you can also set sail on it when the volunteer crew hosts several cruises during the year, including the annual Brews on the Bay— "Two fun-filled days of drinking beer and talking with San Francisco brewers," according to the ship's brochure.

Of course that kind of party behavior might have landed you in the ship's brig during wartime, when the vessel made several important

This vintage World War II vessel is still shipshape.

journeys, including participation in the D-Day invasion of Normandy in 1944. Liberty ships were used to transport important military equipment, supplies, and food to American forces in Europe and the Pacific. Launched in 1943, the *O'Brien* was the only American vessel to return to Normandy for the fiftieth anniversary celebration of D-Day.

That might not have happened if not for a dedicated group of volunteers who rescued the ship in 1978, raised money for its restoration, and donated thousands of hours of labor to restore it to working condition.

If you can't make one of the ship's cruises, you can pay a visit while the ship is docked at Pier 45. Step back in time and tour the ship's interior, including the gun deck, wheelhouse, captain's cabin, and engine room. The ship also contains exhibits, including historic photographs and a stunning diorama of the Normandy invasion.

For information call (415) 544-0100 or visit www.ssjeremiahobrien .org.

Something Funny about This Head Count

The automaton Laughing Sal is a freckle-faced, chubby chuckler with an ample bosom and a gap-tooth smile who bursts into a prolonged, boisterous, phlegm-coated cackle at the insertion of a coin. Drop her a quarter and her arms swing into jerky motion as if she's convulsing with sinister spasms of shrieking laughter. She's equal parts haunting and mirthful, and for years she both entertained and horrified visitors to San Francisco's Playland at the Beach, a seaside amusement park where she was stationed at the entrance to the funhouse.

Playland closed in 1972 to make way for beachfront condos, and it seemed that Laughing Sal's chortling would become a nostalgic lament for those who fondly remembered Playland. Three decades after Playland's demise, officials at Santa Cruz's Beach Boardwalk paid $50,000 to a private collector for Playland's original Laughing Sal and set her up at their beachside park to resume her tittering ways.

Then came a howl of protest from Edward Zelinsky, owner of San Francisco's Musee Mecanique—a palace of antique coin-operated amusements. He countered that he possessed Playland's original Sal and that it was part of the Musee's display. Then another San Franciscan, David Cherry, went public with a story about how he had witnessed Sal's head being ripped off its body at Playland's closing and that he had acquired the decapitated skull for his collection. Richard Tuck stepped into the controversy by announcing that he was opening a tribute to Playland in El Cerrito to be called Playland Not at the Beach, which would include a reproduction of the park's original Laughing Sal.

The conflict raised the question of who had the real Laughing Sal, and whether four laughing heads were better than one. Meanwhile, the various Sals seem unfazed by all the hullabaloo as everyone waits to see who will have the last laugh in this mystery.

Just who has the original Laughing Sal remains a mystery.

3

West

For much of *San Francisco's early history, its western section was mostly a forgettable swath of sandy terrain smothered in fog. But the development of Golden Gate Park and surrounding neighborhoods changed all that. By the early twentieth century the city's western communities developed an identity all their own.*

The area boasts one of the city's finest cultural attractions in Golden Gate Park, which offers many forms of outdoor recreation and plenty of curiosities as well. Take the park's herd of bison, a staple here for more than a century. The state's most famous bear once lived here, too, a grizzly named Monarch later immortalized in a menacing pose on the state flag.

The park is filled with statues, even though the park's founder was adamantly anti-statue. Go figure. The Japanese Tea Garden is a nice spot to experience serenity, and it serves up a bit of history as well. The tea garden is the only remaining exhibit from the city's Midwinter Exposition of 1894.

While Golden Gate Park grabs all the attention, a mere speck of a park not too far away is equally magnificent. Cayuga Park offers magical walking paths and dozens of hand-carved figures made by the park's longtime gardener, who transformed this tiny open space into a miniature land of wonder.

And in a city that loves its ice cream, here is where you'll find shops offering some of the San Francisco's most exotic frozen flavors, including purple yam, spinach, and macapuno.

Looking Out from Within

You may wonder why anyone would want to step inside a darkened room to view an image of what was outside that room, when you could easily see what was outside the room by simply not going into the darkened room.

That's the perplexing proposition offered by the Giant Camera, a longtime San Francisco attraction behind the Cliff House that draws people by promising stunning 360-degree views of what is outside it.

The Giant Camera is actually a camera obscura, a device often credited to an invention by Leonardo da Vinci in the sixteenth

Sixteenth-century technology provides modern-day thrills.

67

century. Many were built in the United States in the early twentieth century. A few remain, but San Francisco's is the only one in America still in its original location.

It was built in 1946 by Floyd Jennings and connected to the Play-land at the Beach amusement area. The building was redesigned in 1957 to look like a giant camera with its lens pointing to the sky. The building's pyramid top contains a rotating mirror that reflects images through special lenses that magnify and focus those images onto a curved and round viewing table inside the building.

Since the building is perched right at the beach, the views here include that of Seal Rock, Ocean Beach, and the many tourists wandering around the Cliff House area. True, while you could simply stand outside the building and pan your own head to see the same sites, there's something magical about seeing the clear images projected onto the large viewing table in the darkened confines of the Giant Camera. There are advantages as well, including being able to stare directly into the sun. A popular viewing time inside here is at sunset.

The Giant Camera has stared down several moves for its demolition and was finally awarded protected landmark status in 2001.

The attraction includes a holograph gallery of framed images hanging on the walls inside. Giant Camera, located at 1096 Point Lobos Avenue, is open from 11:00 a.m. to sunset on clear days. It's best to call ahead (415-750-0415) to learn about that day's viewing times.

Step Right into Nowhere

Visitors to Lloyd Lake in Golden Gate Park come upon a surreal scene. On the edge of the lake sits an ornate and imposing entranceway to a house. That's it, though: a door, and no house behind it. The fancy entrance opens up to a sloping hillside with trees and vegetation.

This marble-columned portico presents itself as a perplexing sight in an otherwise tranquil place. Yes, you could enjoy the scene,

This doorway tells a story about San Francisco's past.

perhaps even break out a picnic, if you could just figure out the meaning of that imposing doorway to nowhere.

Some might chalk it up to another provocative public art piece—a pretty good guess in a city that has plenty of those. But this is actually a significant memorial dedicated to one of San Francisco's darkest times.

This doorway led somewhere once. It was part of a Nob Hill mansion built for the Alban Towne family in 1891, and the entire abode once stood at 1101 California Street. That is, it did until April 18, 1906, when the city was struck by a massive earthquake and fire.

Thousands of homes were destroyed in the devastation, including many Nob Hill mansions. But as residents wandered through the neighborhood, they were struck by the sight of the Towne family's entranceway, which had somehow withstood the blow. A famous photograph was taken of the standing portico that showed the smoldering ruins of the city through the framed structure, and the doorway became an icon for survival after the earthquake.

The portico was donated to the city in 1909 and brought to its current location in Golden Gate Park. The only public memorial to the 1906 disaster, it's now called Portals of the Past.

You can find Lloyd Lake just west of the intersection of John F. Kennedy and Crossover Drives. If you approach the portico you'll discover a small plaque that states the significance of the entranceway to San Francisco's history.

The Last Great Bear

California's state flag features a ferocious bear loping across a green mound. The bear image on the state banner is actually a tribute to a real bear named Monarch that lived in San Francisco for more than twenty years after he was captured in 1889 and brought to the city by publisher William Randolph Hearst.

Monarch, weighing a regal 1,000 pounds, was the last grizzly bear ever found in California. He was exhibited first at Woodward Gardens and then in the city's first zoo, in Golden Gate Park. When he died in 1911, Monarch's mount became the model for the bear on the state's flag, adopted the same year.

Where the Buffalo Don't Roam

Golden Gate Park is a refreshing urban oasis of lush meadows, small lakes, ball fields, and museums. That much you expect. What comes as a surprise to many visitors is the discovery of a herd of bison in a small paddock area at the western end of the park's John F. Kennedy Drive.

The massive beasts with the bulbous heads always seem to be having bad fur days. In fact, an earlier herd was exiled to nearby San Bruno in the 1980s because it had become too sickly and "scruffy" in appearance, according to news reports. A new herd was bought from a meat company that normally supplied a local restaurant known for its buffalo burgers.

**Bison have been hanging around
Golden Gate Park since 1891.**

Spared becoming an entree, you'd think the new herd would kick up its hooves and savor life a bit. But these wooly animals don't live up to their lore as wanderers. They mostly shuffle about munching pine needles or pose majestically while kneeling on the ground in a slumbering stance. Still, even while stationary, they are quite a sight.

The park's bison represent a dogged preservation effort begun in the late nineteenth century after the American buffalo, which once numbered in the millions, had almost been wiped out by hunters. A male and female were brought to the park in 1891 and quickly got busy, and the herd's numbers grew steadily. The first two buffalo were named Benjamin Harrison and Sarah Bernhardt, beginning a tradition of naming the buffalo for well-known public figures. Later animals were named for former mayors of San Francisco, and others took the monikers of figures from Shakespeare.

The San Francisco Zoo, charged with caring for the animals, says that more than 500 calves have been born at the park in the more than one hundred years the bison have been in residence there.

Getting Pumped Up about Historic Pumps

When San Franciscans decided in the late nineteenth century that they needed an urban recreational area to rival New York's Central Park, they couldn't have picked a more challenging terrain to build it on. The verdant landscape of gardens, trees, meadows, and fields now known as Golden Gate Park was mostly a wasteland of shifting sand when the park was first planned.

The city built two towering windmills along the coast to provide the massive amounts of water needed to support vegetation to tame this inhospitable environment. They constructed the Dutch windmill in 1902 to the north and the Murphy windmill in 1905 to the south. Together these mills pumped more than 70,000 gallons of water an hour from underground wells for the next two decades as the park took shape. Then the mills were shut down and left as photo props for the snapshot-taking tourists who began flocking to the popular park.

Golden Gate Park's two historic windmills helped turn the park green.

While the Dutch windmill received some cosmetic work in the 1980s, the mills were in a state of severe disrepair by the start of the twenty-first century. Then a major renovation effort was finally begun. The endeavor is so sincere that parts from the Murphy windmill were shipped to a company in the Netherlands for restoration, a family-owned operation that has been in the windmill business since 1868. The plan now is for the massive Murphy windmill to be fully restored to begin spinning and pumping water sometime in 2010. At last, it seems, the city is finally paying needed attention to the hardworking machines that helped shape one of its greatest treasures.

These Artworks Are Just Plain Garbage

San Franciscans tossing away old shoes, used wrappers, or worn tires may just think they're taking out the trash. In reality, because of one of the country's most unique artist-in-residence programs, they also may be collaborating on an art project. Since 1990 the SF Recycling and Disposal Company, which runs the city dump, has hired several San Francisco Bay Area artists to fill the unique position of artist-in-residence at its recycling plant and trash-collection site.

While it may not seem like a prized opportunity to some, these artists get unlimited access to all the city's garbage to use as raw material for their creative imaginations. The position does have a decided upside, such as the use of a studio on the company's forty-four-acre facility and access to all kinds of fancy equipment, such as cranes, welding apparatus, power tools, and a glass kiln. There's also an honorarium.

Artists selected to the program spend three months on-site sorting through trash and creating their works, often fanciful sculptures. One artist even used items such as discarded zippers and tape to make a formal evening gown and trashed Venetian blinds to construct a tiara. There is a reception for the artists at the end of their stint.

Works created through the program are displayed in what has to be one of the most unusual sculpture gardens in the country—a hillside setting at the dump. There are also scheduled tours of the garden where you get the chance to talk with the artist in residence. For more information call (415) 330-1414, or view some of the works online at the company's Web site: www.sunsetscavenger.com.

Out of This World and into a Cone

There's no place to sit, the lines are usually long, and there are plenty of other places more conveniently located to get frozen treats in this ice cream-loving city. So why is Mitchell's Ice Cream so popular? It must be the macapuno. That's sweet coconut, in case you've never been there.

Macapuno is just one of the many exotic fruit and vegetable flavors offered here daily on a menu that challenges conventional wisdom about ice cream. Can purple yam be an ice-cream flavor? Yes, it can. It's bright purple, mildly sweet, creamy, and satisfying. Other unusual flavors here include jackfruit, lychee, and buko, or baby coconut. There are seasonal ice creams too, such as fresh cantaloupe in summer, pumpkin pie in fall, and eggnog in winter.

"Cantaloupe is very popular. People start asking for it in February," says Larry Mitchell, who started the shop in 1953 with his brother, Jack. Funny thing was, Larry admits he didn't know much

Mitchell's Ice Cream is home to many exotic frozen flavors.

about making ice cream back then, even though his family had run a dairy in the same neighborhood back in the 1800s. So a dairy salesman spent a week showing him the ropes. It still took some years before the shop's popularity really took off in the 1960s, if somewhat by a fluke.

The Mitchells had a friend who was importing mangoes; they bought a bunch and turned them into ice cream. The frozen mango flavor was a hit with the neighborhood's growing Filipino population. Soon the Mitchells were experimenting with all kinds of otherworldly fruit and vegetable flavors in the kitchen of their shop, where all their ice cream is made daily. They've never looked back at chocolate or vanilla since.

The shop is still a family operation, although Jack has long since retired. Larry still maintains his usual hands-on management style, one reason there are no franchises. It would be too hard for him to keep an eye on every store. You'll just have to drop by 688 San Jose Avenue (415-648-2300) to taste for yourself.

Other exotic offerings in town include Bombay Ice Creamery at 552 Valencia (415-431-1103), which offers flavors such as fig, saffron rose, ginger, and cardamom, and Polly Ann's at 3142 Noriega Street (415-664-2472), which is known for vegetable-flavored ice creams such as spinach and tomato. You won't know whether to eat it from a cone or melt it over a pizza.

It Fits to a Tea

The Japanese Tea Garden in Golden Gate Park screams serenity. Well, okay, more like it whispers. It's an oasis of calm with idyllic set pieces, including several gardens, picturesque bridges, ponds, Japanese monuments, and pleasant walking paths. As its name suggests, the Tea Garden also serves up a great cup of tea.

For all its present aura of tranquility, the Japanese Tea Garden has its roots in a macho display of urban one-upmanship more than a century ago.

The Japanese Tea Garden dates to the late nineteenth century.

It seems that San Francisco leaders who had attended the Chicago World's Fair in 1893 returned home with an urgent determination to mount their own boastful display of civic pride. In record time, the city mounted its own world's fair a year later with the opening of the 1894 Midwinter Exposition in Golden Gate Park.

The fair, with an Eastern theme, was a roaring success, and the Tea Garden was a big part of that. Today it remains as the only surviving exhibit from that long-ago exposition. The Tea Garden, the oldest public Japanese garden in the United States, is open daily from 9:00 a.m. to 6:00 p.m.

The Gardener's Imagination Ran Wild

Cayuga Park has some serious drawbacks, including its tiny size and limited recreational opportunities, consisting mostly of a simple grassy ball field and concrete tennis and basketball courts. The park's most glaring disadvantage is its location—right under roaring BART trains that thunder by on elevated tracks.

So it's a good thing the park had one major asset in the form of its city gardener, who toiled here for more than twenty years before retiring in 2008. In that time he transformed what was a gritty urban open space into a wonderland of color, imagination, and lush vegetation.

Using a chisel and chainsaw, Demetrio Braceros created dozens

Gardener Demetrio Braceros carved up a tiny but beautiful city park.

of hand-carved wooden sculptures in vivid color and fanciful design. Some of his works include whimsical figures of people and creatures. For others he wrote out his message of hope and peace.

Braceros also applied his gardening skills to fill out the park's once-desolate landscape with fruit trees, herbal plants, and all kinds of vegetation. He created magical paths along the park's edge that give visitors the feel of walking through an enchanted forest.

The sculptures are scattered through the park. Some are tall totems that stand like quirky trees, adorned with figures of birds and mythical creatures. Other sculptures are perched on trees along hidden paths and are pleasant surprises for visitors exploring the park's grounds.

Since Braceros retired, neighbors have organized to maintain his work and prevent vandalism to the sculptures. You can see all of his creations by visiting the park, located at the west end of Cayuga Avenue, where it intersects Naglee Avenue.

A Dogged Preservation Effort

The dog had his day all right, but it wasn't a very good one. Disastrous, in fact. The 7-foot-tall fiberglass dachshund, a mascot for a once-popular chain of hot dog stands known as Doggie Diners, had tumbled from atop a pole during a windstorm and landed on its pointy schnoz. The literal nosedive occurred April 1, 2001, and police officers at first chuckled at the reports, thinking they were an April Fool's joke. But stories of the plummeting pup were true, yet another twist in what was already one of the country's strangest historical preservation efforts.

Doggie Diners had their day too, but that was a generation ago, when there were about two dozen of the hot dog stands throughout San Francisco and Oakland. All of them featured the grinning, candy apple–red dachshund spinning on a pole out front. The dog sported a blue polka-dotted bow tie and a white chef's hat.

The chain fell on hard times and closed in 1986. The doggie heads were eventually sold to private owners and taken down—all except one outside a restaurant on Sloat Boulevard at Forty-sixth Avenue, a former

A lot of time and money went into saving this big dog.

Doggie Diner. Preservationists had puppy eyes for the last doggie still standing and stirred up a fierce political battle, barking at city officials to declare it a protected landmark. That effort failed, but the city agreed to take up ownership of the orphaned dog. City officials were making plans to shore up its perch when it fell over a year later in a storm.

The city, along with private donors, raised $25,000 to restore the dog to prime condition, including fixing up its smashed snout. During a gala ceremony it was put back in place in June 2001. The wide-eyed pup now flashes a silly grin at passersby and gazes out at the horizon—not a landmark yet, but a dog with quite a tale nevertheless.

A Looming Bust behind Every Tree

John McLaren didn't want statues placed in Golden Gate Park. He would have preferred that park visitors enjoy its natural beauty without man-made distractions.

You'd think his opinion would have carried the day, since McLaren is known as the "Father of Golden Gate Park." But in this case civic leaders thought father didn't know best. They filled the park with more than three dozen statues and monuments, turning the park into a veritable outdoor art museum.

Stroll the park grounds enjoying the trees, lush vegetation, rolling paths, and open fields and soon enough you'll encounter a monumental statue of a bronzed historical figure gazing meaningfully off into the horizon. The figures range from the well known to the obscure. Some make sense, while others make you ponder just what they're doing there.

Take, for example, the large-scale tribute to the apple cider press, located near the de Young Museum. A leftover from the city's Midwinter Exposition of 1894, it features a muscular young man clad only in a strategically placed loincloth, straining to pull a lever of the press while a boy toils with another part of the press at his feet.

Then there's the bronze baseball player from the 1880s, holding a metallic ball and tensed in a position more appropriate for executing a discus toss. You'll find him poised for action outside the tennis courts along John F. Kennedy Drive.

There's the *Pioneer Mother,* standing proud near the park's Pioneer Log Cabin, with the following dedication: "Over rude paths beset by hunger and risk she pressed onward toward the vision of a better country."

Elsewhere there are statues of Beethoven and Verdi, Shakespeare and Cervantes, a Roman gladiator and a Buddha.

And yes, in a final insult to the park's creator, there's a statue of John McLaren himself.

There are dozens of statues in Golden Gate Park, even though the park's founder didn't want any.

This Is About It

San Francisco's trademark frozen treat has been a favorite since it was invented in 1928. It's a frosty concoction consisting of a disk of vanilla ice cream sandwiched between two oatmeal cookies and coated with chocolate. No taste bud would argue with that winning combination of flavors and texture.

The only mystery here is its name: It's-It.

One explanation is that its creator, George Whitney, knew right away he had nailed it, and exclaimed: "It's it!" Another plausible tale has Whitney attending a cow race where the winner was named It. Whitney heard someone ask who had won the race, and the reply came back, "It's It." Whitney liked the sound of that and decided it made a great name for his ice-cream invention.

For many years It's-Its were only sold at the Playland at the Beach amusement park at Ocean Beach. When the park was demolished in 1972, It's-Its were made by hand and sold from a small beach storefront.

Today a factory in Burlingame (sorry, no tours) produces the frozen treat by the thousands daily. For ordering information go to www.itsiticecream.com.

Giving a President the Treatment

In keeping with the longstanding tradition of naming important structures after U.S. presidents, San Franciscans went to the polls in 2008 to bestow an honor on George W. Bush.

Only this wasn't much of an honor, since the building in question was a sewage treatment plant.

Supporters of Proposition R, who concocted the plan while

★ ★

drinking in a bar, thought that naming the Oceanside Water Treatment Plant after Bush was a fitting tribute, since the group felt that
the forty-third president had made a mess of things. While many in
this heavily Democratic city might have agreed with that sentiment,
the proposition was soundly defeated.

Publicity over the proposal brought attention to the award-
winning treatment plant, located off the Great Highway near the
San Francisco Zoo, sparking interest in the facility. Tours are available
for San Francisco residents only by calling (415) 695-7341.

A Great Place to Drop In

Back in the late '60s, it seemed that every young American was donning tie-dyed clothing, piling into VW vans plastered with peace
stickers, and heading to ground zero of America's counterculture movement—the intersection of Haight and Ashbury Streets in San Francisco.

The Haight was as good a place as any to "turn on, tune in, and
drop out," as Timothy Leary urged this restless generation to do.
There were cheap rents, plenty of groovy folks, and exciting events,
such as the Human Be-In at nearby Golden Gate Park in 1967, the
year that ushered in the Summer of Love.

Another attraction was the Haight's vibrant music scene, which
included legendary local talent such as the Grateful Dead, Jefferson
Airplane, and Janis Joplin.

The times have certainly a-changed for the former hippie enclave.
The Grateful Dead are long gone from Haight-Ashbury, and the clos-
est thing you'll get to them now in this neighborhood is a Cherry
Garcia ice cream cone at the Ben & Jerry's on the corner. The Dead's
flophouse from the '60s still draws visitors at 710 Ashbury Street.

Businesses such as the People's Cafe at 1419 Haight Street and
the Bound Together Anarchist Collective Bookstore at 1369 Haight
pay tribute to the neighborhood's counterculture roots.

The Haight-Ashbury Free Clinic, first opened in 1967 near the corner
of Haight and Clayton, thrives today. The Red Victorian Movie House at

1727 Haight still offers funky seating and serves popcorn in big bowls.

Trendier, more upscale boutiques dominate the area today, even though one or two head shops remain, harkening back to an earlier time of pipe-dream bliss.

The People Who Lived in Cars

In the late 1800s San Franciscans came up with a unique way to recycle old city railcars that were once employed as horse-drawn transportation but had outlived their use. People purchased them for twenty bucks each and hauled them out to the beach area south of Golden Gate Park's western end. Then they found all kinds of new uses for them: clubhouses, offices, restaurants, and even homes.

By the early 1900s, there were more than fifty families living in these old railcars, and the community became known as Carville. Some homes were sparsely furnished; others were more elaborate.

More people showed up in 1906—refugees from the fire and earthquake—and Carville began to take on a more permanent community status, with sidewalks and utility hookups.

But more traditional development of the Outer Sunset turned public sentiment against Carville, culminating in a 1913 public burning of one of the railcars being used as a clubhouse.

Carville diehards tried to blend in, building more traditional frameworks around their railcar homes, hoping to disguise them. Carville eventually faded away, although today one or two homes in the Outer Sunset are sometimes discovered when remodeling projects reveal that trademark rectangular shape, uncovering a remnant of the city's lost car neighborhood.

Fun in the Fog

If you're planning an outing to Ocean Beach, you can probably leave the sunscreen behind. Nature will take care of that for you, as the sun will most likely be shielded by a thick layer of moist fog and heavy clouds.

Chances are slim anyway that you'll have any skin exposed to the elements. Typical beach attire here is heavy pants, sweatshirts, hats, and sometimes gloves.

First-time visitors to San Francisco's largest beach might expect to find a sun-drenched stretch of sand packed with people lounging in skimpy outfits or frolicking in the waves. These novices receive a fast lesson in geography. Those kinds of cheery beach scenes are most likely found on postcards, or farther south. Here in the frosty north, the beach scene takes on a whole new image.

Even in summer, air temperature at Ocean Beach is usually in the 50s. Add in the moist air and wind, and it will feel colder. Much colder.

And if you're thinking about a casual swim, forget about it. The waves are ferocious. The water is bitter cold, thanks to a condition known as upwelling, where the outgoing tide churns up frigid water from the ocean depths and brings it to the surface.

And yet Ocean Beach is a fine place for an introspective walk, a brisk jog, kite flying, or extreme surfing. It's a perfect spot to walk your dog or take a romantic sunset stroll.

Ocean Beach covers a wide expanse of sand that runs from the Cliff House to Fort Funston. If you crave a more traditional beach outing, try your luck at one of the city's other sandy spots, China Beach (at Sea Cliff and Twenty-eighth Avenue) and Baker Beach (end of Battery Chamberlin Road). Although tiny, both beaches are more likely to have sunny weather. And even if they don't, both afford spectacular views of the Marin Headlands and the Golden Gate Bridge. So bundle up and warm to the unique experience of a day at the beach in San Francisco.

Don't forget to pack your winter coat for a
San Francisco beach outing.

★ ★

Everything Here Is in Ruins

Looking out on the site of the Sutro Baths today, it requires some imagination to picture how magnificent the attraction once was. Okay, lots of imagination. Because all that's left now are scant ruins—mostly crumbling concrete walls.

The baths were once a glorious sight. Adolph Sutro built the massive glass, iron, and wood structure for $1 million and opened it in 1896. At the time, it was the world's largest indoor swimming facility and included seven pools, six of which were filled with salt water. More than 10,000 people could enjoy the pools at the same time and play around with trapezes, slides, and diving boards.

The baths proved costly to maintain, and in 1937 the structure

A few crumbling walls are all that's left of a once-great San Francisco attraction, the Sutro Baths.

was turned into a skating rink, which also failed. Amid plans to develop the site for apartments, the baths burned down in 1966.

The ruins, just north of the Cliff House, are a popular place to hike and explore, albeit with caution. Enjoy the coastal views; then close your eyes and conjure up the ghosts of what once was one of the city's most wondrous attractions.

An Inside View of the Great Outdoors

It may seem strange while you are in the midst of one of the world's great outdoor recreation areas, Golden Gate Park, to think of stepping indoors to experience even more scenes of nature. That is, until you enter the park's Conservatory of Flowers.

The conservatory is a white palace of a greenhouse devoted to showing off the world's most exotic plants. It opened in 1879 during a period when San Francisco and other cities felt compelled to give their citizens a little taste of the nature that was being lost amid the expanding urban environment. It's now the oldest wooden conservatory remaining in the United States.

Fires, boiler explosions, winter storms, and even the Great Depression have threatened the conservatory through the years, but it has always bounced back. A major $25 million overhaul completed in 2003 should secure the conservatory's future through the next few decades.

With its Victorian styling, the conservatory offers visitors a window into an older world of quiet contemplation. Its rooms are bursting with plants and flowers that brush up against visitors as they pass through its narrows pathways. There are four main viewing areas devoted to vegetation from highland tropics, lowland tropics, aquatic plants, and potted plants. Each room has its own colors, scents, and climate.

The conservatory boasts the oldest and most complete collection of highland orchids in the United States. It also showcases a variety of nature's oddities, including a more than one-hundred-year-old

The Conservatory of Flowers offers Victorian-era recreation.

giant philodendron nicknamed Phil and water lily plants with leaves that grow up to 6 feet in diameter and are capable of supporting the weight of a small child.

Step carefully around the conservatory's section of meat-eating plants—ingenious living things that exhibit all kinds of shrewd techniques to lure, trap, and ingest insects.

With its central dome rising 60 feet into the air, and its more than 10,000 window panes, the conservatory is hard to miss at 100 John F. Kennedy Drive. It's open Tuesday to Sunday from 9:00 a.m. until 5:00 p.m. For more information call (415) 831-2090 or visit www .conservatoryofflowers.org.

South of Market

The width of *a street separates South of Market from North of Market, but the two sections of the city seem worlds apart. Things are just artier South of Market—and more extreme. It's as though moving south of Market Street gives people license to exhibit more outlandish behavior. An anything-goes atmosphere is the norm here.*

South of Market is where you'll find the world's largest leather bondage festival—and a museum dedicated to cartoon art, as well as an entertainment venue inside a bustling Laundromat.

South of Market is known for its many street murals, with passageways such as Balmy Alley a veritable outdoor museum of art, with every wall a colorful display.

South of Market is also where baseballs sometimes soar over the right field wall of the home park of the San Francisco Giants and land in the bay. There they float briefly until they are scooped up by one of the eccentric boat people who patiently wait for a "splashdown" souvenir, one of South of Market's most prized trophies. It's a rare thing indeed, just like the entire South of Market area, one of the most unique urban zones in the country.

Wacky Tricks with Furniture

Some people might take discarded old furniture and appliances to the junkyard. Artist Brian Goggin took a different route when he gathered thirty pieces of cast-off items he found in the street and then cleverly attached them to the side of a building to make them look as though they had just been hurled from it.

The public artwork looked like a crazy freeze-frame of suspended animation, that precious moment just before everything—the lamps, bathtub, television set, couch—would come crashing down to the street below.

This is one way to move out of an apartment.

Except everything stayed right where it was.

The project was completed in 1997 on the outside of a four-story building at the corner of Sixth and Howard Streets. Goggin titled it *Defenestration,* which means the throwing of something from a window.

That's an apt description. Items clinging to the side of the building include a bed, tables, and a refrigerator. The furniture and appliances have a worn, almost tortured human quality to them, as though they can sense their own downtrodden state. The grandfather clock appears to be grimacing in an agonizing half-twist as it perches precariously out one window. A tattered green sofa looks as though it is leaping out a top-story window in a final act of despair.

It is fitting that the building itself was abandoned. With no people inside, it's no wonder the remaining furnishings were making a dive to get out too.

A protracted battle over the future of the building between its owners and the city appeared to be finally resolved in 2009, with the city taking it over by eminent domain and paying the owner $4.6 million. The transfer leaves the fate of the sculpture exactly where the work's hurled furnishings have been for years—up in the air.

This Money Maker Needs a Good Retirement Plan

When San Francisco's coining operations moved to a new facility in 1937, the city's old mint building assumed a decidedly unglamorous moniker: the Old Mint.

Not a respectful title for a monumental structure that had played such a pivotal role in the financial history of San Francisco, as well as the nation.

The Old Mint isn't even the city's oldest mint—the city first began making coins in 1854 in a different site located in what is now Chinatown. However, with the riches being generated by the gold rush, that first mint was quickly overwhelmed and a newer operation opened in 1874 at Fifth and Mission Streets.

★ ★

This newer mint, the one now called the Old Mint, was quite an operation. By 1877 it was churning out almost two-thirds of the nation's gold and silver coins, producing $50 million worth that year alone.

The Old Mint proved a valuable asset when the city was struck by the 1906 earthquake and resulting fire. It withstood the disaster and was the only financial institution able to open as recovery began. The mint's $200 million in reserves were used to aid the city's recovery.

The Old Mint also maintained an impressive portion of the nation's wealth, housing a third of the country's gold reserves.

The Old Mint was once a big moneymaker.

But in 1937, when the city's minting operations moved to Duboce Avenue and Buchanan Street, the Old Mint began a slide toward oblivion. On the outside, the Greek Revival building still maintained its imposing look. But behind its stone walls, the mint was crumbling.

There were repeated calls for it to be torn down, including a proposal in the 1970s that it be razed to make way for a downtown campus of San Francisco State University. Even though it had been declared a National Historic Landmark in 1961, by the 1990s the building was overrun by rats.

There are now big plans for the Old Mint. In 2003 the federal government sold the building to the city for the price of one silver dollar that had been minted at the building in 1879. Now money is being raised to renovate the building and open it as a history museum, a move that would vastly improve the fortunes of this once great moneymaking palace.

Where Redwood Trees and Cable Cars Stand between You and Ten Pins

Ah yes, the majestic scenery of Yosemite. It just makes you want to . . . bowl? While turning Yosemite National Park into a bowling alley would make naturalist John Muir turn over in his grave, it's a reality of sorts at the Metreon Entertainment Center. The latest in computer technology meets up with the traditional low-tech world of recreational bowling at an attraction called HyperBowl.

HyperBowl offers the opportunity to turn settings such as the streets of San Francisco and Tokyo, a pirate ship, and even hallowed Yosemite park into virtual bowling alleys that show up on a big screen. Bowlers here bend over a real bowling ball and then frantically spin and turn it to control a virtual ball that rolls along the screen toward computer-projected pins. In the San Francisco game, for example, bowlers have to navigate their ball down and then up major hills while avoiding urban obstacles such as buildings, fire hydrants, and moving cable cars. Players also have a limited time to get the ball to the pins or they score a zero. The only similarity to this and real bowling is the scoring.

San Francisco's HyperBowl was the first offering of its kind in the country, although it's now catching on elsewhere and is available as a home version as well. Strike out for 101 Fourth Street to get the full original experience.

Pumping New Life into a Faded Beauty

When Levon Kazarian heard that the St. Francis Fountain was for sale in 2002, he was stunned.

"I couldn't believe it," Kazarian remembers. Considering the shape it was in, others may have found it hard to believe that Kazarian and partner Peter Hood actually bought the venerable confectionary and ice-cream parlor.

"It was beautiful, you could see that, but it was dying," he says. The whole place had a "faint ammonia smell to it," he recalls, along with a ceiling painted "Pepto-Bismol pink." The place was in severe disrepair.

So Kazarian and Hood set to work and restored the St. Francis to its original glory, along with a few changes. They made it more of a diner, knocking out a storeroom to build a complete kitchen. There are plenty of sandwiches, salads, and breakfast items on the menu, as well as standard fountain treats such as ice cream, egg cream sodas, and even a Guinness float, which consists of Guinness Ale and vanilla ice cream.

"We claim to be the oldest soda fountain left in the city," Kazarian says of the St. Francis, which first opened in 1918. It would be hard to argue, since the place has a real old-time feel, with wooden booths and Formica countertops inside and elegant neon signage outside.

To enhance the throwback ambience, a candy cabinet from 1920 offers nostalgic sweet treats such as Necco Wafers, wax lips, candy buttons, Bottle Caps, and more. For an even greater time-warp experience, you can pick up assorted trading cards from television shows from the 1970s and 1980s.

As you might expect, there's a lot of history attached to the

The meals are served fresh at the city's oldest soda fountain.

place, but the most significant to San Francisco is that the St. Francis was a hangout for Tony and Vic Morabito, who often lunched here while developing their plan to launch the city's first National Football League team in 1946, the 49ers. Apparently the deal was sealed with Bank of America representatives in a back booth at the St. Francis over a meal of open-faced sandwiches.

If you'd like to bite off a bit of this historic beauty, drop by the St. Francis at 2801 Twenty-fourth Street. It's open Monday through Saturday from 8:00 a.m. until 10:00 p.m. and on Sunday from 8:00 a.m. until 9:00 p.m. Call (415) 826-4200 or visit www.stfrancis fountainsf.com for more information.

There Was Plenty Right about This Lefty

Young San Francisco baseball fans in the 1930s and 1940s headed to Seals Stadium for Lefty O'Doul Day for Kids, when youngsters were admitted for free to root for the city's Pacific Coast League team. Kids received a bag of peanuts and a small baseball bat autographed by O'Doul and then scrambled for free baseballs that O'Doul chucked into the stands.

Yes, Francis "Lefty" O'Doul is one of the city's most beloved sports heroes, and it's not just because of the free peanuts.

A native San Franciscan, O'Doul had a great professional career, twice winning the batting championship. He managed the San Francisco Seals of the PCL from 1935 to 1951. The team played in a downtown stadium bounded by Bryant, Sixteenth, and Alameda Streets and Potrero Avenue; the stadium was demolished in 1959.

O'Doul made dozens of trips to Japan to promote baseball starting in 1931 and is credited with sparking that country's interest in the sport. A colorful character, he was often spotted around town wearing a green suit, leading to his nickname, "the Man in the Green Suit."

O'Doul is honored today by a bridge that runs along Third Street near the San Francisco Giants stadium. His restaurant, Lefty O'Doul's, remains as well at 333 Geary Street. For more information call (415) 982-8900 or visit www.leftyodouls.biz.

Where Comics Come to Clean Up Their Act

Stand-up comedy is hard enough under the best of circumstances. You know, like performing at an upscale comedy club.

That's not challenging enough for a bunch of beginning San Francisco comics who prefer to hone their comedic skills in the confines of a Laundromat.

Yes, a Laundromat. With the scent of detergent and softener in the air, and as underwear and other soiled apparel churn away in banks of washers and dryers, these up-and-coming comics deliver punch lines, tell stories, and otherwise do their best to coax yuks from an audience that might be more interested in how its laundry is coming along than in laughing.

This new spin on laundry and entertainment is the venue known as the Brainwash Cafe and Laundromat. Brainwash hosts weekly open-mic comedy nights as well as other performances, including poetry readings and live music.

A full-service cafe serves up a variety of foods, from hot and cold sandwiches to salads, pastas, and all-day breakfast items. Doing the laundry has never been this fun. Some people come just for the food and entertainment, without lugging in any dirty clothes, which seems strange, considering they are walking into a Laundromat.

Of course if doing the laundry is on your agenda, there are plenty of washers, dryers, and supplies on hand. There's even a service where you can drop off your clothes and have your laundry cleaned for you.

If this seems like a laundry where you can get down and dirty, head over to Brainwash at 1126 Folsom Street. It's open Monday through Thursday from 7:00 a.m. until 10:00 p.m., Friday and Saturday from 7:00 a.m. until 11:00 p.m., and Sunday from 8:00 a.m. until 10:00 p.m. To find out who's performing when, call (415) 255-4866 or check out www.brainwash.com.

A Valiant Performance under Pressure

San Francisco is the only city in the world that has honored a fire hydrant for heroic duty. Some residents gush with pride at the mention of the humble hose attachment, located at the intersection of Church and Twentieth Streets. It was here, in the aftermath of the great earthquake and fire of 1906, that firefighters made a dogged stand against a hell storm of flames heading for the Mission District. When every other hydrant failed, this reliable fireplug supplied a steady stream of water that aided the efforts to subdue the blaze and save the neighborhood.

That's heady stuff for a hydrant. The plug has been elevated to the

★ ★

status of Golden Hydrant and is a symbol of civic pride and the city's spirit to rise from the ashes of that catastrophe. On every anniversary of the quake, remaining survivors gather at the hydrant to coat it with a fresh topping of golden paint. A plaque imbedded in the sidewalk tells the story of the champion plug, ensuring that its great deed won't be forgotten. A note to passing dogs: Don't even think about it.

This is one heroic hydrant.

Buy Them Some Peanuts
and Life Jackets

For some San Francisco Giants fans, the best seats in the house aren't even in the house. They're not even seats really but flotation devices, such as kayaks, canoes, rafts, inner tubes, and speedboats. During each home game at the Giants' downtown baseball stadium, a crafty group of boaters gathers in a narrow channel outside the park's right-field section. It's a vantage point that affords nice views of the San Francisco Bay—but not even a glimpse of the action on the field.

No matter to this crew. They set their sights on landing a most rare catch in these frigid waters—a home run ball hit out of the stadium and into an area of the bay known as McCovey Cove, in honor of former Giants slugger Willie McCovey.

Home runs hit by a Giant over the park's 24-foot-high wall and into the bay are called splashdowns, and they are prized souvenirs to these floating fans.

There are only a handful of splashdowns each season, which means that boaters outside the stadium have a lot of time on their hands. Most come prepared with ice chests of drinks and grills to barbecue up floating feasts as they party away while following the game on portable radios, televisions, and cell phones.

When a home run does make a splash, there's a mad dash for the ball, with some people diving into the water and others trying to maneuver their craft into retrieval position to scoop up the ball with fishing nets. Then the long wait begins anew.

Cameras outside the stadium capture all the action in McCovey Cove, and it has proven to be a popular sidelight at games. The exposure has made some Cove regulars celebrities around town. There is a downside, though. When a home run is hit, some right field fans toss a baseball into the water just to watch the mad scramble for it. When the ball is found, the boater has a momentary feeling of success until the ball is examined to reveal what's written on it: "Sucker."

★ ★

His Career Spanned Lots of Bridges

Joseph Strauss is most famously known for designing and promoting San Francisco's Golden Gate Bridge. And why not? It's truly one
of the world's most beautiful ways to cross over water, a crowning
achievement for Strauss.

Before he conceived of the Golden Gate, Strauss had a busy career
designing and building lesser known works, including dozens of
spans known as bascule bridges for their use of weights to raise the
roadway.

**Before he designed the Golden Gate Bridge, Joseph Strauss
started small, like this Fourth Street Bridge.**

Far from the shadow of the Golden Gate you can see two of these bridges in the China Basin section of the city.

The Fourth Street Bridge, also known as the Peter R. Maloney Bridge, opened in 1917 and is the oldest operating drawbridge in the state. The Third Street Bridge, commonly called the Lefty O'Doul Bridge, opened in 1933 and is located near AT&T Park, home of the San Francisco Giants.

Both bridges were designed by Strauss and his Bascule Bridge Company, and cross the Mission Creek Channel.

One Long-Standing Mission

While California missions certainly have a controversial side, there is no disputing the historical significance of Mission Dolores in San Francisco. It's the oldest building in the city, as well as the only remaining intact mission from that period of California's past.

Twenty-one missions were built in California, stretching from San Diego to Sonoma, and constructed mostly in the late eighteenth century. The Spanish set up a chain of missions to establish settlements in Alta California ahead of Russians moving down from the north and to convert local Indian populations to Christianity.

Mission Dolores, also known as Mission San Francisco de Asis, was founded in 1776. It's a small church with subtle decorative features, including an artful main altar, built in Mexico and brought here in 1796, as well as colorful side altars, redwood roof supports, and columns painted to look like Italian marble.

Visitors stepping into the narrow wooden church are transported back to the early days of mission life. The grounds include a small museum that contains artifacts such as incense holders, holy water containers, and religious vestments.

There's also a small cemetery, the only remaining one in the city. Burials took place here until the 1890s. The headstones are in various states of decay. Some are faded and cracked with barely legible engravings, while others have fared better over time. The cemetery,

Something old, something newer: historic Mission Dolores, with the more modern church on the right.

with its flowers and greenery, is actually a peaceful place to spend a few moments. It contains an Indian memorial in the center that is a thatched hut, a tribute to the native populations that sometimes endured harsh treatment while housed at California missions.

A newer basilica was built right next door to the original church and completed in 1918. It's much bigger and contains beautiful stained-glass windows. Services take place in both churches.

The mission, located at 3321 Sixteenth Street, is open daily, except for religious holidays, from 9:00 a.m. until 4:00 p.m. Call (415) 621-8203 or visit http://missiondolores.org/old-mission/visitor.html for more information.

Where Time, and Greasy Spoons, Have Stood Still

Nowadays the people you encounter in the Embarcadero section of San Francisco are upscale condo dwellers and office workers, or gourmet diners heading to a nearby trendy eatery. It wasn't always this way, though. The docks here were once the domain of, well, people associated with dock work, like longshoremen and sailors.

That gritty past is all but obscured by urban renewal, except for two notable exceptions: two blue collar shacks that once served up cheap and hearty meals to the dock workers of old.

San Francisco has not one but two historic dockside eateries, both named Java House.

The Java House and Red's Java House stand out more like living museum exhibits than places to dine. Yet these tiny wooden buildings right on the water's edge are really popular, no-frills restaurants offering bargain-filled menus.

The Java House opened in 1912 and is the oldest eatery on the Embarcadero. It features a humble menu of breakfast items and sandwiches, all prepared in a tiny kitchen and grill area in plain view of the main indoor dining section. There's a small side room with a tiny television set, as well as an outdoor patio where you can enjoy a meal while listening to sounds of seagulls and staring out at the bay.

Story has it that two brothers once owned the Java House. The one with red hair then opened a second shack farther up the way, calling it Red's Java House. The menu here is similar to the original Java House, with offerings of breakfast, burgers, and beer, which you can eat in an inside dining area or outside on simple tables and chairs overlooking the water.

The Java House at Pier 40 (415-495-7260; www.javahousesf.com) and Red's Java House at Pier 30 (415-777-5626) are also popular on game days for the San Francisco Giants, who play at nearby AT&T Park.

Tapping into a Rich History

While most people associate northern California with winemaking, the San Francisco Bay Area actually has a much longer connection with the more humble craft of beer production. Dating to the gold rush era, there were dozens of breweries churning out barrels of a West Coast potable known as "steam" beer, a nickname that connoted the way the lager was made without ice and quickly fermented. When barrels of steam beer were tapped, they supposedly emitted a trademark puff of foggy vapor.

Most of these breweries eventually went out of business as America's taste for beer drifted to lighter, mass-produced fare. All except one, that is—San Francisco's Anchor Brewing Company.

While the brewery dates to the 1860s, it was given the Anchor label in 1896. Through the years it moved around a lot in the city; it hit on hard times as well. The brewery was saved in 1965 by Fritz Maytag, he of the family known more for its washing machines. Only Fritz was interested in making a different kind of suds.

Maytag not only revived the Anchor brewery and its trademarked steam beer but is also credited with leading a national revolution in microbreweries. Anchor Brewing now produces seven different beers, including a seasonal Christmas Ale. All brews are painstakingly hand-crafted in copper kettles, keeping alive San Francisco's great tradition of making beer.

Visitors are invited to tour the facility although reservations (415-863-8350) should be made well in advance, because the tour is popular (after all, it comes with a tasting at the end). The brewery is located at 1705 Mariposa Street, and you can get a lot of information online at www.anchorbrewing.com.

A Street Fair Gone Wild

On one hand, the Folsom Street Fair offers the kind of sights and entertainment you'd expect at, well, most any other street fair: jugglers, music, dunk tanks, food and drink, vendor booths, and a lively outdoor atmosphere.

And then the Folsom Fair takes it to another level entirely. Because here you're likely to encounter public floggings, scantily clad dancers writhing in metal cages, near-naked adults engaged in a robust game of outdoor Twister, and hundreds of people outfitted in a wild assortment of latex and leather outfits.

The Folsom Street Fair is an annual coming-out party for the leather-loving bondage crowd, bringing fetish fans out of the dungeon and into broad daylight, spilling on to five blocks of Folsom Street. It's the world's largest festival of its kind.

The festival had humble community beginnings in 1983, growing as a natural extension of the dominant gay leather scene along

Folsom Street. Now it's gone decidedly mainstream and commercial, drawing hundreds of thousands of people each year from around the world and raising thousands of dollars for several charities.

Some festivalgoers are gawkers with cameras who just want to see just how far San Francisco's tolerance for alternative lifestyles really goes. Others just strap on various leather garments (the skimpier the better it seems) and jump right in to join in the celebration.

The street fair is the crowning moment of Leather Pride Week, which leads up to the event. In addition to the public displays of bondage rampant along the street during the fair, there is also live music, and vendors offer tools of the trade, including lots of leather items, assorted lotions and oil, and whips and chains.

If you dare, head over to Folsom Street between Seventh and Twelfth Streets on the last Sunday of September. The less adventurous can pay a visit to www.folsomstreetfair.org.

Masters of Exterior Decorating

San Francisco probably leads the nation in the number of murals. Blank walls here cry out "Paint me!" to anyone with a brush and an artistic vision. More than 600 murals adorn walls, garage doors, fences, and any other available outdoor public space that can be turned into a painted canvas. Cruise a few city blocks and you'll feel as though you're in an art gallery instead of outdoors along a city street.

The highest concentration of this unique art form is in the city's Mission District, clearly the heart of San Francisco's mural movement. The first murals began appearing here in the 1970s along Balmy Alley between Harrison and Twenty-fifth Streets, painted on garage doors and apartment walls. Murals have since spread to every conceivable space in the neighborhood, including along the walls of taquerias, churches, and corner stores.

The murals here are boldly drawn in vibrant colors and are mostly massive works expressing powerful themes. For example, on the

Blank walls are not permitted in the mural-happy Mission District.

corner of York and Twenty-fourth Streets, there is a blue-toned tableau depicting provocative images of police oppression. Other works celebrate the neighborhood's Latino culture or are more spiritual and religious in nature.

The Precita Eyes Mural Arts Center at 2981 Twenty-fourth Street has helped foster the mural movement here, offering classes and tours. You can go on a guided walk with someone from the center and see seventy-five murals in only 6 blocks.

The group also sponsors the annual mural awareness month each May, an event that features painting contests and a live mural performance where an artist will create a mural in an afternoon. For more information contact the group at (415) 285-2287 or visit them online at www.precitaeyes.org.

On the Wrong Side of the Slot

A neighborhood on the "wrong side of the tracks" is understood to be a less-desirable place to live. In cable car San Francisco, that expression was changed to "South of the Slot," a derogatory label for the community south of Market Street. Cable cars once ran along Market Street and were connected through a slot in the street. South of the Slot contained the city's poorer neighborhoods filled with factories and warehouses.

The neighborhood name was later changed to the more gentrified-sounding South of Market and is now abbreviated as the utterly cutesy SoMa, more reflective of the area's upscale trend.

A Serious Look at the Funny Papers

Saturday morning cartoons and the Sunday comics are good for a few laughs. Do they also qualify as art? That's what some cartoon fans believe. They've created a Louvre of Looney Tunes known as the Cartoon Art Museum—the only museum in the country dedicated to cartoon art in all its forms.

The museum began in 1984 as a traveling show but now, thanks to an endowment from *Peanuts* creator Charles Schulz that was more than just peanuts, they've got a permanent space. The museum contains more than 6,000 original pieces of cartoon art, a research library, a bookstore, and a classroom for lectures.

It's okay to laugh as you study some of the comic-strip panels hung on the walls like fine art, framed and illuminated with track lighting on an expanse of white wall. But, perhaps swept up by the

⋆ ⋆

studious museum setting, you may also find yourself considering the artistic and cultural merits of, say, a *Calvin and Hobbes* panel, or even one from the *Family Circus.* Framed cels from animation feature classics such as *Snow White* and *Pinocchio* are easily admired in this environment and appreciated for their artistic appeal.

The museum tackles the weighty world of political cartoons too. One special exhibit highlighted the powerful satiric work featured in *The Wasp,* a political weekly featuring cartoons published from 1876 to 1897. The cartoons displayed presented scathing attacks on political and cultural figures of the day, such as Leland Stanford and Oscar Wilde.

Laugh and learn at the Cartoon Art Museum.

The museum likes to profile cartoonists and present the scope of their work, such as an exhibit on Johnny Gruelle. While best known for creating Raggedy Ann and Andy, he was an illustrator who did much more. The museum exhibited some of his other works, as well as vintage dolls, toys, and animation art based on his characters.

A visit to the museum at 655 Mission Street should foster a greater appreciation for cartoon art.

For more information call (415) CARTOON (227-8666) or visit http://cartoonart.org.

They're Growing Their Own

A small square of urban land surrounded by tall buildings and in the shadow of a noisy freeway hardly seems like the place to plant some vegetables. Or fruit for that matter, and even flowers. But at the Alice Street Community Gardens, it's not just about the Swiss chard, leeks, and potatoes. This unusual community garden is a bit more like physical and spiritual therapy for the dozens of senior citizens who come here to till their tiny plots of land and grow their produce.

The gardens, owned by a community agency known as the Tenant Owned Development Company, or Todco, offers seniors living in the area a chance to plant whatever they want in wooden soil containers that measure 4 by 6 feet. There are more than 160 plots of land allocated in the gardens, and there's a long waiting list for seniors eager to try their green thumbs out if given the chance.

Ron Cousino, who manages the gardens, says that their most important aspect is that the gardens help keep participating seniors feeling young. The gardening work gets them outside, requires physical activity, and promotes socializing with other gardeners. Many of the elderly gardeners here often trade growing secrets and recipes among this ethnically diverse group.

The gardens don't just put food on some tables but also offer a great place to visit for everyone else. It's a pleasant oasis amid the

★ ★

Seniors show off their green thumbs at these urban gardens.

surrounding urban sprawl, complete with lush scenery. Many people come here just to relax on park benches, eat their lunch, or just collect their thoughts.

The Alice Street Community Gardens is open every day during daylight hours—just follow the sound of the singing birds to the intersection of Bonifacio and Lapu-Lapu Streets.

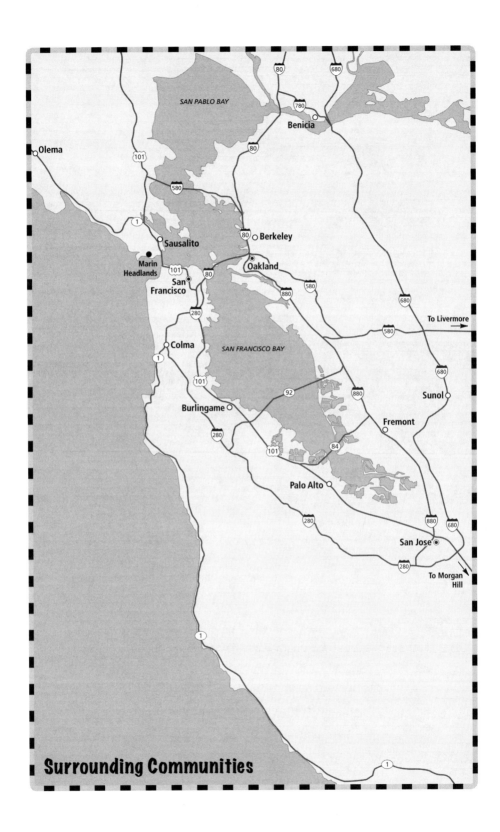

Surrounding Communities

5

Surrounding Communities

Being a suburb of San Francisco is a little like being that underachieving sibling who doesn't get enough attention. You try harder to get noticed. But not to worry for the many communities that make up the San Francisco Bay Area. They have plenty going on in their own right. There's plenty here worth seeing and knowing about, and it's all very curious and sometimes downright astounding.

Like the little light bulb that could—it's burned continuously since 1901. And the house that's shaped like an obscure marine organism.

There's an annual UFO Expo in San Jose, the largest of its kind in the world. A children's theme park in Oakland predates Disneyland—and probably gave Walt Disney ideas about how to design his own magic land. There is plenty of wartime history to be found in some of the most tranquil settings on the planet. You'll also find one of the largest and best reptile stores in the country.

While San Francisco boasts some of the most eccentric thinkers in the world, no one there ever thought of appointing a dog as mayor. But the quaint folks in the quaint town of Sunol did. The pooch did a mighty fine job in office too.

★ ★

A Spitting Image from the Past

Benicia

Benicia certainly has bona fide historical roots. It briefly served as the state capital from 1853 to 1854. And word of a gold discovery at Sutter's Mill first circulated at a Benicia general store in 1848, setting off a massive rush of fortune seekers and leading to California's statehood.

Benicia is also linked with a less-illustrious saga in American history, involving a short-lived and miserably unsuccessful experiment with camel transportation. The U.S. military briefly employed several dozen camels imported from the Near East in 1856 in hopes that the humped creatures would excel in arduous treks through the Western deserts and badlands. These were heady days for camel supporters, who envisioned the charge of a camel cavalry and even a camel express for delivering mail. In the end the beasts proved too burdensome to handle, and in 1864 the herd was sent to Benicia for auction.

Historians aren't clear on exactly what happened here, but the camels probably spent a couple of months at the Benicia Arsenal, a historic place in its own right. The arsenal, opened in 1849, was one of the West's earliest military posts and served through several wars before closing in 1965.

Legend has it that the camels were stabled at two warehouses at the arsenal before they were sold off; these building are now called the camel barns. While the camels' stay here was short, they haven't been forgotten. A historical museum at the camel barns pays tribute to them, and the city began hosting annual camel races in early summer as an additional link to its dromedary past. For more information, trek over to www.beniciahistoricalmuseum.org.

★ ☆ ★ ☆ ★ ☆ ★ ☆ ★ ☆ ★ ☆ ★ ☆ ★ ☆ ★ ☆ ★ ☆ ★ ☆ ★ ☆ ★ ☆ ★ ☆ ★ ☆ ★ ☆

Mothballed but Not Forgotten
Benicia

The harbor tugboat the *Hoga* began its U.S. Navy service in 1941 and was stationed at Pearl Harbor when the Japanese attacked. The *Hoga* helped extinguish many fires that day and rescued several stranded American seamen. The *Hoga* served admirably throughout the rest of World War II and the Korean War and was eventually loaned to the city of Oakland, where she served for five decades as a fireboat.

The aging but dependable tug was placed "out of service" in 1996 and charted a course for Benicia, the final resting place for dozens of retired naval vessels. Benicia is home to the Suisun Bay Reserve Fleet, a storage facility that harbors about one hundred decommissioned military craft, including guided missile cruisers, submarines, barges, oil tankers, and Coast Guard icebreakers. This site is one of three in the United States maintained by the maritime branch of the U.S. Department of Transportation.

It's sometimes called the mothball fleet. Sure enough, many look like they belong in storage, with rusted out exteriors and interiors stripped of working parts. Other ships are regularly maintained as part of the Navy's Ready Reserve Force, which means they could be rushed into service in an emergency.

Beneath their corroded shells is a lot of history, and former shipmates of particular vessels have adopted these aged craft in hopes of preserving them. One former Suisun Bay vessel, the SS *Jeremiah O'Brien,* made it out of mothballs and is now docked at Pier 45 in San Francisco as a floating museum.

Another beloved vessel is the *Glacier,* an icebreaker that went on dozens of Arctic and Antarctic missions. Volunteers from a group called the Glacier Society, including former crewmen, are restoring the ship and raising money to find a permanent home for it. It's the same story for the 325-ton *Hoga,* the last surviving ship from the Pearl Harbor attack. Supporters hope that such a historic vessel won't suffer the ignoble fate of being cannibalized for spare parts and tossed on the scrap heap.

★ ★

Your Cold-blooded Pets Await

Berkeley

There are those who would run screaming at the first sight of a spider, snake, or even a newt. And then there are those who just can't wait to see these and other, often scaly, creatures that conjure up visions of a prehistoric world.

For the latter, the place to be is Berkeley's East Bay Vivarium, one of the oldest and largest herpetological stores in the country. It's a veritable reptile zoo, except that all the creepy crawlers here—from boa constrictors to tiny frogs to tarantulas—are for sale as pets. Even if you don't want to walk out with a snake, spider, or lizard, it's fun

How much is that lizard in the window?

to wander through the narrow aisles, stare into the glass cages, and gawk, even if it might make you feel a bit squeamish.

The store has all the accessories you need to care for the new reptilian member of your family, including terrariums, food, and even jungle vine ("it's bendable and twistable!"). There are even live mice for sale at the front counter to feed to your snake. You'll find them in translucent plastic drawers and they come in different sizes, depending upon the appetite of your pet.

Some of the reptiles here are even available to rent for birthday parties, including "Fluffy," the black throat monitor.

The East Bay Vivarium is open from 11:00 a.m. until 7:00 p.m. Monday through Friday and on weekends from 11:00 a.m. until 6:00 p.m. So summon up your courage and head over to 1827-C Fifth Street in Berkeley or, if you prefer to keep your distance, order online at www.eastbayvivarium.com.

A Call for the Wild

Berkeley

Berkeley has always been more of a state of mind than a real place. Oh sure, it's a city with a mayor, police department, and streets and stuff, but it's also a symbol for ultraliberal ideals and outright zaniness. It's a place where all politics are worldly.

Fittingly, Berkeley was the scene for the birth of the free speech movement in the 1960s. So when locals organized a parade and festival with the provocative title "How Berkeley Can You Be?", it was pretty obvious that myriad way-out acts and personalities would answer the challenge to celebrate the city's wacky heritage.

The event, begun in 1996 and held each fall, routinely showcases outlandish offerings such as a precision lawn-chair brigade, a naked marching group advocating peace, pregnant women promenading with synchronized contractions, and an Italian cafe that catapults giant meatballs onto a colossal plate. Participating politicians don't dare travel this liberal-minded parade route in anything but a solar-

★ ★

powered vehicle. There are protests and political satire too, including a group called Not in My Backyard, whose members carry signs that read: IF YOU BUILD IT, WE WILL COMPLAIN.

John Solomon, a local restaurateur, developed the parade and festival as a way to celebrate the city's well-earned reputation for tolerance and diversity. He also hoped to draw people to the city's sometimes-neglected University Avenue corridor, where the parade begins.

For information on the event, parade over to www.howberkeley canyoube.com.

A Feeding Frenzy

"One, two, three—latch!"
Following these instructions, more than 1,000 mothers gathered in the Berkeley Community Theater in August 2002 to soothe their hungry babies and, more important, set a new world's record for mass breast-feeding.

The collective nursing not only quenched a lot of infant appetites but also eclipsed a previous mark set by 767 women in Australia. The final Berkeley tally was 1,128 suckling babies, according to event organizer Ellen Sirbu, a city nutritionist.

Sirbu acknowledged that the event was a way of one-upping, lactation-wise, the Australian group. But she also wanted to spotlight the benefits of breast feeding and encourage other American cities to hold similar events. So now Berkeley, home of the Free Speech Movement in the 1960s, is out in front on another vital social movement.

In addition to establishing the breast-feeding mark, Berkeley also set another perhaps inadvertent milestone: biggest mass baby burping.

Just Try and Blow This House Down
Berkeley

The most unusual aspect of the Tsui House on Matthews Street in Berkeley is not the way it looks. And that's saying a lot, because as home designs go, this one is pretty far out there.

With its fins, elliptical shape, and porthole windows, the circular dwelling reminds people of some kind of sea creature. And even that's off target, because its creator, Emeryville architect Eugene Tsui, says the design is actually based on a tardigrade—a microscopic organism that lives in water or damp ground and seems impervious to any attempt to destroy it. Knowing this, you can see why people prefer to call it the Fish House. It's just much easier that way.

This odd house looks like it washed up from the beach.

Tsui calls it the safest house in the world, and since he built it for his parents, you can understand why safety was a priority.

Earthquakes? The home just absorbs the shockwaves and moves on. Fire? The circular shape is designed to have air flow around it, so flames don't spread inside the house. And special water jets placed on outside walls put out any flames that even begin to threaten. Flooding? The home features a drainage system that includes pipes to immediately remove any sudden water buildup.

The home even repels termites with its unique cement block and Styrofoam foundation.

The 2,000-square-foot, three-level home, which sits on a block of mostly one-story bungalows built in more traditional fashion, certainly catches one's eye from the street. It has four bedrooms, three baths, a carport, and a whole bunch of special features. Like "breathing" windows that allow air to circulate in and out, but not insects.

The home was completed in 1995 at a cost of $250,000 and after much public debate. It includes built-in cabinets and shelves and a suspended spiral ramp inside. There are no stairs—a requirement specified by Tsui's parents.

Tsui calls the home Ojo del Sol, or the Sun's Eye. The house, at 2747 Matthews Street, certainly shines a light on one indisputable fact: Things sure are different in Berkeley.

A Hefty View from a Bridge

Berkeley

The Berkeley Big People, two monumental sculptures that span the pedestrian and bicycle bridge that crosses I-80, certainly live up to their name. They are big. And in a city famed for its protest culture, it's no surprise that they are controversial.

The perplexing public art was commissioned by the city to be a gateway symbol that would capture the spirit of Berkeley. Created by Emeryville artist Scott Donahue and installed in 2008, the mammoth artwork is both stupendous and stupefying.

The two 30-foot-tall sculptures, perched on each end of the bridge, feature 12-foot-high figures representing the city's people and activities.

Prominent on the east side work are two angry-faced protestors holding up blank, framed protest signs, seemingly growing out of the neck of a wheelchair-bound figure who slouches beneath them. Behind them, a woman plays a violin using a metal bow. Smaller relief figures sculpted below their colossal counterparts feature other

This public art in Berkeley is not to be missed.

★ ★

scenes of protest, including one of Mario Savio leading the free speech movement at the University of California at Berkeley in the 1960s.

On the west side work, devoted to scenes of recreation and nature, two long metal poles sprout from one man's eyes, each pole formed at the other end into a figure of a bird, while nearby a dog leaps to catch a metal Frisbee.

After the work was installed, it stopped many bicyclists and walkers on the bridge as they tried to decipher the meaning of the work—the largest public art project in the city, at a cost of nearly $200,000. It would probably stop drivers along the freeway below, too, if not for the onrush of traffic from behind.

Even the city's arts coordinator was quoted in the *San Francisco Chronicle* as saying, "It's exquisitely done—but if some people don't like it, that's okay." The *Chronicle*'s art critic called the work "a new black eye on the already battered face of public art in the Bay Area." Others have voiced support for the work, calling it inspiring and praising it for celebrating the energy and protest culture emblematic of the city and the university.

One thing is clear: Berkeley's Big People are impossible to miss— just head for the pedestrian bridge at the end of Addison Street.

The Bare Truth about the Limits of Free Expression
Berkeley

The Naked Guy came to class with his books. He even donned sandals. He just didn't wear any clothes.

The Naked Guy was a University of California at Berkeley student in 1992 named Andrew Martinez, and he really tested Berkeley's famed tolerance for far-out lifestyles. The ultimate lesson of Naked Guy's educational experience was that there is such a thing as going too far, even in a place with a rock-solid reputation as a liberal-minded community.

Following a student conduct hearing that Martinez attended in the buff, the school expelled him for his unconventional attire. School officials claimed his nakedness was disruptive in the classroom. Hey, at least teachers would know he wasn't cheating on exams.

Then Naked Guy got under the skin of city officials when he showed up as his traditional bare self at a city council meeting. Red-faced council members promptly passed a controversial law outlawing public nudity in 1993. Sure enough, Martinez was the first person arrested under the law.

Open-minded jurors, not wishing to squash anyone's desire to cavort unclothed around town, have been reluctant to convict anyone, making enforcement of the law difficult for city officials. After many failed attempts, the city finally earned a conviction in 2000 of two members of a group of professional nudists known as the X-Plicit Players.

The Berkeley-based group hasn't been convinced to dress up despite the ruling. They continue to host several events around town to commemorate nudity, including the annual Nude and Breast Freedom Parade, held in Berkeley's People's Park. The event celebrates the "liberation of the body from boring fashion," according to the group's Web site, www.xplicitplayers.com.

Adding a Little Kick to Your Rice
Berkeley

Kudos to the first person who thought of turning rice into an adult beverage. Rice has always been an important food staple. But turning it into a refreshing alcoholic beverage? That's inspiring.

The tradition of making rice wine, or sake, dates back hundreds of years in Japan, where it is a popular drink. In the United States beer is king, but that hasn't stopped the Japanese company Takara Sake from doing its part to develop an appreciation for rice wine here in America. The company opened a sake brewing facility in Berkeley in 1982 that includes the country's only sake museum. To make the experience even sweeter, there's a free tasting room.

Before you taste, you need to learn a little about sake, which is actually closer to beer than wine in how it is prepared. During the shogun period in Japan, there were more than 30,000 sake breweries.

The key ingredients, according to a video of sake history that plays in the airy tasting room, are good rice, great water, and a suitable climate—all of which are readily available in the Bay Area. The company uses rice from the Sacramento Valley, water from the Sierra Nevada snowmelt, and takes advantage of Berkeley's cooler climate to produce its product.

A wood-paneled exhibit hall adjacent to the tasting room, illuminated by several overhead skylights, displays many tools and

These tools of the trade turn rice into a refreshing beverage.

equipment used in the making of sake. There are also artifacts and photos that demonstrate sake making from the nineteenth century.

Strolling through the exhibit area is bound to make a person thirsty, so visitors can then make their way back to the tasting room to sample four different types of sake made at the Berkeley plant. Takara also produces plum wine.

To experience just how good rice can taste, head over to the museum and tasting room at 708 Addison Street, which is open daily from noon to 6:00 p.m. For more information call (510) 540-8250 or visit www.takarasake.com.

Flipping Their Lids over Vintage Candy Dispensers
Burlingame

Gary and Nancy Doss planned on selling computers. Really they did. In fact, the sign on their store still says COMPUTER SPECTRUM. But, as Gary points out, "We haven't sold a computer in eight years."

It's all because they were struck by Pez mania. Soon after they opened the computer store, they decorated it with a few Pez dispensers from their collection, thinking that customers would enjoy looking at them. Boy, did they ever. Soon people were dropping by not to look at computers but to gawk at their impressive collection of Pez dispensers. Eventually their computer store was reborn as the Burlingame Museum of Pez Memorabilia.

You know Pez dispensers, the slim plastic canisters developed to dole out the tiny brick-shaped candies known as Pez. Pez candy, created in 1927 as an aid to help people quit smoking, took off in the United States in the early 1950s when it was sold with cartoon-head dispensers. Today vintage Pez dispensers are highly collectible, making the Pez museum a popular stop with Pez enthusiasts.

"Everybody seems to have fond memories of Pez. It's a cartoon toy and a candy, all in one. Unlike other products, when you're finished you've got something left over to keep," Gary says.

Some vintage Pez containers now sell for hundreds of dollars, while new ones retail for a buck or two. Gary says that the museum carries about 500 different dispensers, from popular ones featuring characters from *The Simpsons* to a rare one from the 1960s known as the Luv Pez, which looks like a giant eyeball in a hand. They recently acquired one of the rarest Pez containers of all, the Make-a-Face Pez, which was quickly recalled from stores because the company was concerned about the small parts posing a safety hazard for kids. Gary says the museum now has every Pez dispenser ever made.

In 2007 the museum unveiled the world's largest Pez dispenser, a towering marvel at 7 feet, 10 inches tall that looks like a snowman and holds close to 6,500 candies. Museum visitors can browse vintage Pez dispensers displayed on old toothbrush racks and also purchase Pez memorabilia in the gift shop, including T-shirts, coffee mugs, and related toys.

For more information, surf to http://spectrumnet.com/pez or call (650) 347-2301. Or head over for a closer look at 214 California Drive.

Land of the Grave
Colma

Being a resident in the tiny town of Colma just south of San Francisco has its privileges, such as lots of free services, including cable TV, tickets to sporting events, and summer camp for kids. There's also a golf course, card club, and scenic views. As the city slogan says, "It's great to be alive in Colma."

It's great to be alive, yes, because the overwhelming majority of those who reside here are not. Colma is a necropolis, the final resting place of an estimated two million souls. The living population numbers around 1,200. That makes Colma a unique community—the only one in America where the dead outnumber the living. And in Colma, it's not even close. That's why the city has many morbid nicknames, including "City of the Dead," "City of Souls," and "City of the Silent."

I see dead people ... lots of them.

Colma's incorporation in 1924 resulted from a ban on burials in San Francisco due to rising land values in the early 1900s. There are seventeen cemeteries in the city's two square miles, and some contain famous folks, including Wyatt Earp, Levi Strauss, and William Randolph Hearst. There's even a pet cemetery that is the final resting place of Tina Turner's dog. Yes, there's plenty of lively history here, and almost all of it can be found underground.

Ego Road Trip

Some drivers long for car accessories such as leather seats, sunroofs, and powerful engines. Others, such as artist and filmmaker Harrod Blank, dream of more esoteric extras for their autos. In Blank's case, that means doors with painted roosters, roofs with TV sets and mailboxes, and bumpers outfitted with assorted musical instruments.

To Blank a car is much more than a way of getting around. It's a vehicle for artistic expression, a creative outlet that's now a bona fide artistic genre, thanks in large part to Blank's promotional efforts.

Blank is revered by followers as the ambassador of the art car movement. Not only has he transformed three of his own vintage cars into rolling canvases but he's also produced two popular documentaries and a book about the art cars and their creators. He's also organized one of the most popular gatherings of auto artists, the annual Artcar Fest in the San Francisco Bay Area—a weekend of art car caravans and related activities.

To promote his first film, *Wild Wheels,* Blank drove one of his art cars to dozens of cities to screen the film, garnering publicity and attention to this unique art form.

His most famous art car is Camera Van, a 1972 Dodge van with close to 2,000 cameras glued to its exterior, including some patterned on the roof to spell "smile". Some of the cameras actually work, controlled from instruments inside the vehicle. Blank has taken hundreds of pictures that capture the wondering stares of people he meets on the road. Another car, a 1963 Volkswagen Beetle, is covered in musical instruments, including running boards made from piano keyboards and cymbal hubcaps.

Blank and other car artists see their work as an expression of freedom by creating cars that become true road maps to their owners' souls.

For more information on Artcar Fest, cruise over to www.artcarfest .com, or learn more about Blank's cars at www.cameravan.com.

A Past That Keeps Cropping Up
Fremont

Once it was nothing special to live on a farm. Just a hundred years ago, in fact, more than half of all Americans did. Feeding the chickens and slopping the hogs were common pastimes. But during the last century, America has seen its agrarian past slip away faster than a greased pig. Now less than 2 percent of Americans reside on a farm, meaning we're a nation of cell phone–lugging city slickers who would be clueless if challenged to milk a cow.

To get a farm fix today, you either have to tune in to see Fox's *The Simple Life*—or head to attractions such as the Ardenwood Historic Farm in Fremont. At this 205-acre spread, life goes on as though the past few decades of technological improvements never happened. The time warp tour includes a blacksmith station, volunteers dressed in nineteenth-century rural fashions, farm critters, wagon rides, and other assorted agrarian experiences long forgotten.

The farm is part of a huge estate once owned by George Patterson, who came west in 1849 to seek gold and ended up becoming rich as a successful planter. Visitors don't just watch; they're expected to chip in with chores, from planting crops to feeding animals. There are many special programs offered throughout the year as well, including fall harvest festivals and a Victorian Christmas celebration. The site also houses a railroad museum.

To learn more, ride a horseless carriage over to 34600 Ardenwood Boulevard, or use the modern convenience of a computer and check out www.ebparks.org/parks/ardenwood.

A Flickering Moment as the Heart of Screenland
Fremont

A town with movie stars, film crews, and frequent cries of "Action!" can only be one place in California … Fremont? While Hollywood has long been synonymous with the film industry, Fremont was an early

★ ★

contender for that distinction. That's due to one hardworking movie company that opened shop in Fremont's Niles district in the early days of film. Dozens of employees of the Essanay Film Manufacturing Company descended upon this small railroad town in 1912 and produced cowboy "one-reelers" at a phenomenal rate. For the next four years the company churned out close to 400 silent films, sometimes making five or six a week.

George Spoor and Gilbert "Bronco Billy" Anderson were the "S" and "A" partners behind the studio. Anderson was the screen's first Western movie star. Essanay scored its first coup with the signing of Charlie Chaplin, who came to Niles and perfected his waddling screen persona here by filming *The Tramp.* The movies made here were mostly shot along Main Street or in nearby scenic Niles Canyon. Residents often served as extras and sometimes offered possessions as props.

When Chaplin left Essanay over a contract squabble in 1916, the company disbanded and the center of the film business moved south to Hollywood, ending Niles's brief reign as a major player. Locals haven't forgotten the studio's or Chaplin's historic connection to the town. There's an annual film festival and Charlie Chaplin Day, when several of the films shot here are presented in a school auditorium with piano accompaniment. For more information visit the town's Web site at www.niles.org.

One Foul Curse

Livermore

Adam Fortunate Eagle Nordwall uttered a dire warning when he stormed out of a Livermore city council meeting in the early 1970s. Because he didn't get what he wanted, Nordwall threatened to put a curse on the city's sewer system. Council members probably viewed the comment as another publicity stunt by the local businessman and American Indian activist. They might have even laughed it off except that within two weeks, sure enough, the city's sewage system most definitely clogged up, just like Nordwall had promised. The incident is

This totem caused a lot of problems for Livermore.

known around here as the Livermore curse, and it's had remarkable staying power.

Nordwall is best known around the Bay Area as a leader of a group of American Indian protesters who took over Alcatraz Island in 1969 and demanded that the federal government give it to all American Indians. The takeover dragged on for months and eventually lost steam; federal agents finally reclaimed the island. Nordwall's book *Heart of the Rock* recounts the episode.

Around Livermore, however, Nordwall is more closely associated with the curse. Nordwall's irritation with Livermore stemmed from what the city did after he donated a totem pole to commemorate Livermore's centennial. The 18-foot-tall pole showed the city's founder, Robert Livermore, sitting under an eagle. City workers chopped it down and encased it in cement before displaying it in a park. Thinking the city had literally performed a hatchet job on his artwork, Nordwall demanded that it be restored. When the city council said no, the famous sewer system curse was uttered.

While the city's sewage system eventually cleared, the curse remains potent.

The curse was revisited in a recent documentary on Livermore in which Nordwall and several city officials are interviewed about the historic incident. Nordwall insists that the curse hasn't been lifted. Sure enough, within a few weeks of the documentary's release, two of the city officials interviewed in the film died, reviving the legend of the Livermore curse.

The Light Fantastic
Livermore

It's not often that a light bulb becomes the center of attention. Almost never in fact, except in the case of one low-watt bulb with extraordinary staying power in a Livermore fire station. The four-watt hand-blown bulb was turned on in 1901 and, except for a rare

Don't ever call this bulb dim.

power outage, has kept right on glowing ever since, making it one heroic light.

More than a hundred years of luminescence have earned the bulb a deserved spot in the limelight. *Guinness World Records* and *Ripley's Believe It or Not* have recognized it as the longest-burning bulb in history. That's pretty heady stuff for a bulb that gives off as much light as a wimpy candle.

U.S. President George H. W. Bush and assorted other dignitaries have written beaming letters in recognition of the bulb's achievement.

But the bulb's fame has been a mixed blessing for fire department personnel. It has brought them worldwide attention for sure. But they sometimes fret about the awesome responsibility of caring for such a celebratory light—and what it would mean if it went out on their watch.

The owner of the Livermore Power and Light Company donated the bulb to the fire department, and originally it hung in a fire department hose cart house. It's been moved twice and was screwed into its present socket on the firehouse ceiling in the mid-1970s.

Visitors are welcome during business hours to view the subtle glow of the bulb's thin carbon filaments. If you can't make it to the station at 4550 East Avenue, you can check out a Web page devoted to the bulb at www.centennialbulb.org. The site features a bulb cam that updates the mighty light's picture every thirty seconds.

Sure It's War, but Check Out the Views
Marin Headlands

Scores of people flock these days to the coastal zone known as the Marin Headlands for splendid recreational outings. With its lush rolling hills and breathtaking views of San Francisco Bay, the headlands are a hiker's paradise and just the spot to cultivate peace of mind.

Or wage war. Yes, this tranquil setting harbors a strong military background dating from the eighteenth century all the way through the end of the Cold War era in the 1970s.

The most striking example of this curious juxtaposition is SF-88—the only restored Nike missile site in the country. At the height of the Cold War there were more than 300 Nike missiles positioned around American coastal areas to protect against a Soviet aerial bombing attack. There were more than twenty of these sites in the Bay Area alone.

A visit to the restored site is a jarring experience. Against the beauty of the coastal hills and stunning coastal views, the site housed the cold instruments of war, including several Nike missiles that could be readied for launch in fifteen minutes.

As battlefronts go, the Nike missile launch
site was a nice place to be.

You can walk right up to one of these missiles and examine it
from top to bottom or take a trip down a missile elevator to explore
an underground storage area. Two sentry posts manned today by
uniformed mannequins add to the chilling experience.

The Nike site is maintained by volunteers, some of them Nike
veterans, who show up on the first Saturday of every month to spin
Cold War tales for visitors. Otherwise the site is open Wednesday
through Friday from 12:30 to 3:30 p.m., except for federal holidays.
Call (415) 331-1453 for information.

The Nike missile site is contained within the Golden Gate National
Recreation Area, considered one of the world's largest urban parks.
It spans 60 miles of scenic coastline in and around San Francisco.
Because of its prime location for civic defense, the park's boundar-
ies contain many historical military sites that visitors can explore. For
more information, it's best to go to the park's Web site at www.nps.
gov/goga and download directions to each location. You can also call
the Marin Headlands Visitor Center at (415) 331-1540.

Bridging a Life Span

Al Zampa once told a reporter that to be a bridge worker you had to be "as surefooted as a mountain goat, agile like a cat, and be able to climb like a monkey." Zampa was all of that during a long career as an ironworker who helped build some of San Francisco Bay's most famous spans, including the Bay Bridge and the Golden Gate.

Mostly surefooted, Zampa is most remembered for one misstep on wet iron he took in 1936 while constructing the Golden Gate. He fell more than 40 feet, fortunately into a net—a modern safety device in this most dangerous and often lethal profession. The net saved his life, but it sagged under his weight and he hit the rocky shore below and broke four vertebrae. Years later he recounted the fall to CBS News and said: "I hit the rocks and bounced. And the first time it didn't seem so hard, but when I came down a second time, whoo—that's when it hurt."

After a lengthy recovery, Zampa got right back on the bridge, yet another indication of his pluck that made him a hero in Crockett, where he spent most of his life. He began working on bridges when he was twenty, working on a cantilever span over the Carquinez Strait. He worked on a second Carquinez bridge, which was completed in 1958. In 2000—at age ninety-four and long retired—he attended a groundbreaking ceremony for a replacement bridge over the Carquinez. He died soon after the event.

That bridge was completed in 2003 and fittingly named in his honor. The Al Zampa Memorial Bridge is a mile long but represents a lifetime for one rare bridge worker, who slipped and fell from the Golden Gate and lived to tell about it.

A Celebration That Creeps Up on People
Morgan Hill

Horror movie directors have long known that casting a big hairy spider to crawl across someone's body or face is a guaranteed way to conjure up a spine-tingling cinematic moment. These on-screen cameos are just one way big spiders, especially tarantulas, have been demonized through the ages. Long ago it was even believed that spiders caused the plague.

Clearing up misconceptions about tarantulas, North America's largest spiders, is one purpose behind the annual TarantulaFest and Barbecue at Henry W. Coe State Park in Morgan Hill. Ranger Barry Breckling, an organizer of the event, insists that native tarantulas aren't creepy at all. They're fragile, docile creatures, and "it would be hard to get one to bite you," he insists. Still, he knows that getting visitors to view tarantulas as cute and cuddly takes some work. The lighthearted nature of the event helps. People can pose for pictures with the spiders crawling over them, or they can go on guided hikes to see them in the wild. There is tarantula-themed food, including bug smoothies—a drink with two straws so that kids can "imitate a tarantula sucking the insides out of a bug," Breckling says. A highlight is a performance by the resident jug band, the Tarantulas.

The timing of the festival coincides with the tarantula's autumn mating cycle, an epic adventure in itself. While tarantulas live underground, when males turn seven they venture from their burrows in search of mates, risking the hazards of the outside world in their quest to coax a female out in the open for a bit of spider hanky-panky. When it's over, the female returns home to hatch her offspring; the male is left out in the cold to die during winter.

While visitors may recoil from seeing tarantulas scurrying about on hiking trails in the fall, there's not a lot to fear, Breckling says. He points out that a spider bite is rarely serious. Meanwhile, it's the spider that is more at risk, more often than not ending up crunched under a hiker's boot.

You can crawl over to www.coepark.org for more information on the festival.

A Real Swell Invention
Oakland

A burning controversy in sports stems not from action on a playing field but rather a feat in the stands. The heated hullabaloo concerns the creation of the wave—that ubiquitous stadium aerobics where cascading sections of spectators rise up, raise their arms, and then sit down, generating the illusion of a wave rippling around the stadium. The wave is now as common at ball games as the stadium hot dog, but it is a modern invention.

The most plausible claim to the wave's debut dates to a baseball playoff game between the Oakland A's and the New York Yankees at the Oakland Coliseum on October 15, 1981. That's when professional cheerleader Krazy George Henderson says he orchestrated the first wave around a stadium.

It began slowly, he recalls. "I knew what I wanted, but no one had ever seen it before," he says. When it stalled, he encouraged fans to boo those who had let the wave die. Spectators finally mounted a robust wave that surged around the stadium. "It was great. The whole place just went nuts," Henderson says.

Henderson, known for his flopping mop of blond hair and trademark drum, says he first conceived the idea when he led cheers in college at San Jose State University. He had done the wave at smaller venues before, but the 1981 A's game marked the wave's premiere at a professional sporting event.

Heated debate swirls around Henderson's claim, and frenzied exchanges have flared up on sports Web sites about the wave's provenance. The University of Washington has mounted a notable challenge, asserting that the first stadium wave originated during a Husky football game two weeks after Henderson's date.

Credible evidence appears to be on Henderson's side. In a 1984 newspaper interview, broadcaster Joe Garagiola, who was announcing the A's-Yankees game in 1981, recalled the wave happening when Henderson says it did. He marveled in the interview: "I had never seen anything like it before. It was super." Henderson's agent, Jon Terry, says he has received a tape of the game from Major League Baseball and the wave is clearly evident during the broadcast.

Henderson is less sure about who came up with the name for the wave. "I have no idea," he admits. "Washington can take credit for that if they want."

Once Upon a Time, Walt Disney Was Here
Oakland

Long before Disneyland, Oakland civic leaders, led by businessman Arthur Navlet, conceived the idea of a storybook theme park for young children. That dream became a reality with the opening of Fairyland in 1950, a magical place that featured storybook sets, puppet shows, and rides and play areas built around the theme of children's stories and nursery rhymes.

Walt Disney visited Fairyland soon after it opened, got ideas of his own, and opened Disneyland five years later in southern California. Disney lured away Fairyland's executive director to join him at his company.

Disney's company went on to live happily ever after, and its connection to Fairyland became obscured by the passage of time. But Fairyland has had its own storybook ending. It fell into disrepair in the 1990s but has since been restored.

You can enjoy Fairyland's charms at 699 Bellevue Avenue year-round; hours vary, depending on the season. Summer hours are Monday through Friday from 10:00 a.m. to 4:00 p.m. and on weekends from 10:00 a.m. to 5:00 p.m.

For more information call (510) 452-2259 or visit www.fairyland .org.

★ ★

Urban Disaster Plus Cow: Coincidence?
Olema

The 1906 earthquake and fire certainly caused widespread devastation in the San Francisco Bay Area. But was the earthquake big enough to swallow a cow? Rumors have persisted for more than a century that indeed it was.

The cow in question died on Payne Shafter's ranch near the town of Olema, south of Point Reyes Station. Witnesses said that the earthquake caused the ground to open up, engulf the cow, and then snap shut, leaving only a tail showing aboveground. Other versions say it was the head and tail still showing, or just the feet. Geologists have said that such a fissure is rare but possible.

The linking of a cow to an urban disaster brings to mind the story of Mrs. O'Leary's cow, falsely accused of starting the great Chicago Fire of 1871. While the story of San Francisco's earthquake cow may or may not be true, it's certain that Shafter's cow didn't start the 1906 earthquake.

An Off-Key Marching Band Out to Pull Your Leg
Palo Alto

Most school marching bands drill endlessly in their quest to perform carefully synchronized halftime shows. Then there are so-called scatter, or scramble, bands, which abhor traditional formations and instead favor screwy, feverish rushes accompanied by much yelling and helter-skelter movements. They are out for parody, not precision, and none more so than the Leland Stanford Junior University Marching Band in Palo Alto, the country's most notorious scatter band.

Stanford's band has constantly pushed the barriers of civility during its infamous routines. A 1990 themed show at the University of Oregon lampooned a sensitive controversy between loggers and environmentalists and featured whirring chainsaws and a formation that projected a dead spotted owl. In 1997 the band presented a parody of the Irish potato famine during a game against Notre Dame that was widely criticized. The band showed up at O. J. Simpson's murder trial in Los Angeles in 1994 and serenaded prospective jurors, a performance labeled as a "new low in tasteless behavior" by Simpson's lead attorney Robert Shapiro.

The group's mascot typifies the band's unconventional approach: It's a tree—and a pretty goofy-looking one at that. It's meant to represent the El Palo Alto pine tree represented on school and city logos. For the band, it's the ultimate anti-mascot.

The tree's taunting behavior has landed it in some hot water, most notably involving confrontations with archrival the University of California at Berkeley. During a basketball game at Stanford's Maples Pavilion in 1995, the tree exchanged wooden blows with Cal's mascot, Oski the bear—a skirmish that was widely replayed on sports shows around the country. In a football game the following year against Cal, the tree was roughed up by some students and had its branches clipped.

It was during a football contest against Cal in a 1982 Big Game that the band had its most humiliating moment. That's when they paraded onto the field in a premature victory celebration, only to get caught off guard as Cal used five laterals to score as time ran out. The winning Cal touchdown came as the player with the ball unceremoniously knocked the band's trombone player right on his horn section.

More often, though, it's the Stanford band that delivers the blow that leaves others flat on their backs.

Mummy Dearest

San Jose

The 1972 Neiman Marcus holiday catalog offered two Egyptian sarcophagi, intended as his and her gift items for "people who have everything." The Rosicrucian Egyptian Museum in San Jose bought them, a purchase that made some sense. Although the folks there don't have everything, they do have 4,000 Egyptian relics, making the museum the largest collection of authentic Egyptian artifacts on display in western North America.

Museum director Julie Scott says they paid about $20,000 for the two coffins, and that price has turned out to be quite a bargain. As the sarcophagi were being delivered, workers discovered that a mummy was inside one of them—and what a mummy he's turned out to be. Museum officials continue to be surprised as they learn more and more about their acquisition.

They originally believed the ancient corpse was a high priest known as Usermontu. An X-ray examination revealed a mysterious screw in Usermontu's knee, which they initially assumed had been inserted in modern times. But in 1996 three orthopedists removed the screw and were startled to discover that it was actually thousands of years old—but remarkably similar in design to screws used in modern orthopedic surgery to reinforce damaged bones. One significant difference was that Usermontu's knee surgery was most likely done after he died to prepare him for burial and the afterlife. News of a sophisticated surgical technique traced back to ancient Egypt created a sensation in scientific circles, and garnered much publicity for the museum.

Now, Scott says, there's evidence that Usermontu might be an even more significant find. In fact, he's probably not even Usermontu and may be one of the missing Ramses Pharaohs, she says. That makes him a star attraction at the museum, which has five other mummies and scores of other artifacts that detail ancient Egyptian life, including a popular walk-through rock tomb.

The museum also offers lectures and other special programs. To glimpse Usermontu, or whoever he is, visit the museum at 1664 Park Avenue. For more information and to view artifacts online, visit www.egyptianmuseum.org.

When Smart People Do Dumb Things

The longtime rivalry between the University of California at Berkeley (Cal) and Stanford University in nearby Palo Alto has inspired a legacy of collegiate foolishness. Students at the two brainy schools plot lowbrow pranks every year designed to humiliate their rivals.

One time the water in a Berkeley fountain turned Stanford red, while a Cal bear print was found stenciled on Stanford's Hoover Tower. Stanford students once stole a stuffed Kodiak bear from Cal's campus. It turned up several days later chained to a fountain at a San Francisco subway station, having suffered the shame of being dressed in a Stanford jersey.

Passions in the rivalry run so high that while the schools boast several Nobel laureates, faculty and students become downright nutty about possessing a simple wooden ax. That's the trophy awarded to the victor of the annual football contest between the two schools. The ten-pound ax with the 15-inch blade was originally bought for about three bucks, but the glory that goes with having it is priceless. Each school protects the ax with elaborate security, often in secret locations. Even so, there have been a few thefts through the years.

Cal students originally stole the ax from Stanford at an 1899 baseball game and then kept it locked in a bank vault for thirty years. Stanford students regained the ax in a 1931 caper aided by the use of teargas.

Here's another thing that seems beneath both elite schools: You know what these deep thinkers came up with as a name for their annual big football game? The Big Game.

Remodeling Redundancy
San Jose

Lots of homeowners have remodeling horror stories. Nothing, though, can top the experience of Sarah Winchester, who began a fix-it job on her San Jose house in 1884 that lasted thirty-eight years and ate up most of her $20 million fortune. She couldn't blame project overruns on a bad contractor. At fault here was peculiar advice Winchester received from a spiritual medium who told her that she could ward off evil forces by never ending construction on her house.

Winchester, heir to the Winchester rifle fortune, believed the seer, who told her that she was cursed because of all the death caused by the "Gun that Won the West." Fearing for her life, Winchester ordered carpenters and assorted contractors to toil away twenty-four hours a day until she died in 1922. The resulting chaotic design includes such oddities as stairways that lead to the ceiling, doors that open onto blank walls, and a cabinet that is actually a passageway to a section of the house. Winchester apparently also communed with spirits for ideas about home design.

When the last nail was hammered into place, the rambling residence contained 160 rooms, 10,000 windows, forty-seven fireplaces, and 2,000 doors. It does have a few attractive amenities, such as Tiffany stained-glass windows, working elevators, and button-operated gas lighting.

The incoherent abode is now a popular tourist attraction known as the Winchester Mystery House. There are guided tours by well-trained docents who have spent some time learning the home's curious floor plan. An adjacent Firearms Museum showcases the rifle that caused so much of Sarah Winchester's consternation. On Halloween and every Friday the thirteenth, there are flashlight tours for those who want to experience the home's haunted side in a spooky, low-light setting.

The home sprawls out at 525 South Winchester Boulevard. Information is available by calling (408) 247-2000 or visiting www.winchestermysteryhouse.com.

It's Out of This World

San Jose

If space aliens were interested in abducting people, they would be wise to pilot their unidentified flying craft over to San Jose each fall, when hundreds of people gather for what is billed as the world's largest UFO convention.

It's known as the Bay Area UFO Expo, and it's been going strong since 1997. While the setting for the two-day annual conference may be the mundane confines of a hotel, the topics explored here are otherworldly. Speakers explore topics such as alien abductions, government cover-ups, and conspiracy theories—and of course strange sightings such as crop circles and flying saucers.

Attendees vary from hard-core believers to the just plain curious. The event is jam-packed with speakers and exhibitor tables, all dedicated to the mysterious world of extraterrestrials.

The expo was founded by Victoria Jack, whose interest in UFOs was sparked by her truck-driving dad, who often came home from long journeys on the road bearing tales of UFO sightings.

If you believe they're out there, get information on the next expo by calling (209) 836-4281. Or visit them on the Web at www.thebayareaufoexpo.com.

A Hull of a Place to Live

Sausalito

Ocean views are a great selling point for any home. When home is a houseboat, there are great views from every window, including those in the bathroom. Which explains a lot about the popularity of houseboat living in Sausalito.

There are more than 400 floating homes bobbing away at more than five different dock areas here, ranging from modest cottages to three-story mansions. There are converted tugboats, barges, and even one home made from an 1889 Pacific Railway Pullman car.

But the most unusual Sausalito houseboat is the floating Taj Mahal,

★ ★

If you lived here, you'd be home now.

a massive white structure made to look like the real building from India.

To get an up-close look at some of these spectacular floating abodes, you can attend the annual Sausalito Floating Homes Tour in the fall, organized by the Floating Homes Association. Call (415) 332-1916 or sail over to www.floatinghomes.org for more information.

Model Behavior
Sausalito

The San Francisco Bay estuary, at more than 1,600 square miles, is larger than the state of Rhode Island. It's easily the largest estuary on the West Coast. So when the U.S. Army Corps of Engineers decided in the early 1950s to build a model of the estuary, the Corps thought on an appropriately grand scale.

The Corps eventually built a massive model of the entire San Francisco Bay that is 1.5 acres in size—the equivalent of two football fields. It's the only three-dimensional model of its kind anywhere, the largest hydraulic water model in the world.

You can feel like a giant here as you tower over San Francisco Bay.

For many years it was a great learning tool for scientists to study just how the interaction of tides, river flows, and water levels affect sections of the expansive bay.

The model was initially needed to evaluate a proposed plan that would have dammed the flow of fresh water into the bay in two key places. The conclusion was that the plan would have disastrous consequences for the ecological health of the estuary, which is a mix of fresh and salt water that supports a wide variety of plant and animal life.

Nowadays, scientists use computer models to study the bay, which is good news for the general public, since the Bay Model has been turned into an educational facility open to the public. A visit to the model provides a unique way to experience the San Francisco Bay.

Visitors first walk up a long ramp filled with exhibit stations containing information about the estuary before entering a small room to view a brief film about the bay and the model. Then they enter the massive model room, which is a truly impressive warehouselike space that contains the scaled-down versions of the various bays that make up the entire San Francisco Estuary.

The Bay Model simulates a complete day of tidal changes every fifteen minutes as shifting water levels are sped up for research purposes. For the casual viewer, the model provides a condensed view of the entire San Francisco Bay Area and landmark structures such as bridges are carefully identified with small markers.

You can feel like a giant as you hulk over sections of the model, located at 2100 Bridgeway in Sausalito. The model is free to view and is open Tuesday through Saturday from 9:00 a.m. until 4:00 p.m. Call (415) 332-3871 or visit www.spn.usace.army.mil/bmvc for more information.

Garage Worship

The garage, that humble storage structure for cars and house junk, has played a key role in the development of several of California's signature companies.

These high-profile successes have fueled a strong belief in the California garage myth—the idea that dreams of a better life can be realized by spending long hours in the garage. Just roll up your sleeves, step over the oil stains and discarded exercise equipment, and get to work. Soon you'll be launching a new product or company that will earn millions—at least, that's how it's worked out for some.

Larry Page and Sergey Brin rented a garage in Menlo Park that became the birthplace of an Internet search firm you may have heard of: Google.

Two famous Steves, Wozniak and Jobs, tinkered for a time in the Jobs family garage at 2066 Crist Drive in Los Altos. They soon came up with a tiny gem of a personal computer called the Apple I. Before you could say "stock options," the Apple Computer Company was born and the two Steves were rich.

The state's most celebrated garage story dates to 1938, when Stanford grads David Packard and William Hewlett, founders of Hewlett-Packard, shunned jobs at established firms and set up their own electronics lab in a garage. The 12- by 18-foot wood-frame shed at 367 Addison Avenue in Palo Alto is now worshipped as the birthplace of Silicon Valley. It's also a state historic landmark.

Hewlett and Packard's first product was an audio oscillator, and they found a willing buyer in someone else who appreciated the value of a garage firm: Walt Disney. One of Disney's first production operations was housed in his uncle's California garage.

And a Dog Shall Lead Them
Sunol

Sunol is a pleasant rural community that boasts a historic railroad station. Nothing much to report here, except that it once elected a dog as mayor.

Community members point out that the mayoral appointment was more of an amusing unofficial gesture. But the black Labrador named Bosco apparently took his job seriously, donning a special vest and badge to lead the town's parades and community gatherings. On the downside, he was open to bribes of beef jerky and biscuits and mostly lounged around the town watering hole.

Mayor Bosco received widespread fame during his term from 1981 until his death in 1994 and even stirred up some international conflict. The Chinese newspaper the *People's Daily,* oblivious to the honorary nature of Bosco's status, used his "election" to rail about the problems with Western democracy.

After his death, the town erected a statue in his honor outside the local post office, and locals opened a bar in his name called Bosco's Bones and Brews at 11922 Main Street. Call (925) 862-0821 or visit www.boscosbonesandbrew.com for more information.

index

index

index

index

index

index

index

about the author

Saul Rubin is an award-winning journalist and full-time journalism instructor at Santa Monica College. He fell in love with San Francisco in 1978 when he first entered the city by driving over the Golden Gate Bridge one typical foggy afternoon. Through the years he's marveled at the city's quirky attractions, including the bison herd of Golden Gate Park and the camera obscura at Ocean Beach. He lives in Los Angeles with his wife, daughter, cat, and dog.